DOM
and to CJ,
My best attempt to chase with words
a path beyond description

———————————————

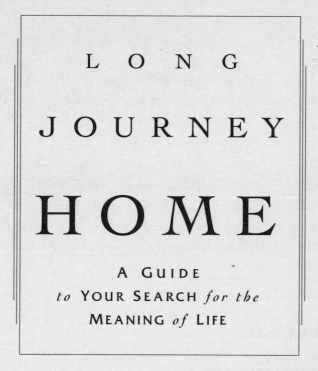

LONG

JOURNEY

HOME

A GUIDE
to YOUR SEARCH *for the*
MEANING *of* LIFE

OS GUINNESS

ZONDERVAN™

GRAND RAPIDS, MICHIGAN 49530 USA

ZONDERVAN™

Long Journey Home
Copyright © 2001 by Os Guinness

First published in the USA in 2001 by WaterBrook Press.

First published in Great Britain in 2003 by Zondervan.

Requests for information should be addressed to:
Zondervan, *Grand Rapids, Michigan 49530*

Os Guinness asserts the moral right to be identified as the author of this work.

ISBN 0-310-25060-9

Quotations on pages 53–56 are from W.H. AUDEN: A Biography © Humphrey Carpenter 1981. Reproduced by permission of the Felicity Bryan Literary Agency.

Published in association with Yates & Yates, LLP, Literary Agent, Orange, California.

Printed and bound in the United Kingdom

02 03 04 05 06 /❖CLY/ 14 13 12 11 10 9 8 7 6 5 4 3 2 1

CONTENTS

CHAPTER ONE

WAKING UP TO THE JOURNEY

❖

"I'm at a point in my life where I realize there has to be something more."

The speaker, a man elegantly dressed, had come up to me after a dinner near San Francisco at which I'd been asked to give some remarks on the modern world's search for meaning. He cut straight to the point, and there was an intensity in his voice that immediately set him apart from the surrounding small talk.

"Like many of my friends around here," he continued, "I've learned a lesson I wish I'd known when I started out: Having it all just isn't enough. There's a limit to the successes worth counting and the toys worth accumulating. Business school never gave me a calculus for assessing the deeper things of life."

Many of the guests at the dinner were eminent names from the world of high finance in the city and the world of high technology in Silicon Valley farther south. Their conversation was flush with the success of the twentieth century's last two decades, a period that witnessed the greatest legal creation of wealth in history, much of it in that very corner of the world.

In my remarks to them, I hadn't uttered the phrase "something more." But in separate conversations with me afterward, no fewer than four people—each with a very different story—used those very words to express their sense of longing. As it happens so often in life, the very things they had striven to achieve turned out to be, once achieved, far less than enough.

I've had many similar conversations in living rooms, classrooms, cafés, pubs, airplanes, and trains across the world. As G. K. Chesterton wrote: "We all feel the riddle of the earth without anyone to point it out. The mystery of life is the plainest part of it." Nothing is more human for people of all backgrounds—for all of us—than a desire to unriddle our life's mystery.

It's often said that there are three requirements for a fulfilling life. The first two—a clear sense of personal identity and a strong sense of personal mission—are rooted in the third: a deep sense of life's meaning. In our time especially, many people are spurred to search for that meaning because they're haunted by having too much to live with and too little to live for. But there are countless other spurs.

This book is for all who, by whatever prompting, long for "something more," who desire to unriddle life, who are pursuing a life rich with significance, who want a seeker's road map to the quest for meaning.

Does that describe you?

FOR HOME, FOR LOVE

When rock star Janis Joplin was a small girl, her mother one night found her sleepwalking outside, moving away from their house.

"Janis, what are you doing?" she shouted as her daughter kept walking.

No reply.

"Where are you going?" she asked.

"I'm going home," Janis said, still farther away. "I'm going home."

Even as a child, Janis Joplin seemed to realize that her parents' house and "the great nowhere" of the ugly oil refinery town where they lived could never be her real home.

Restless, always restless, she later was devoured by a loneliness so great that neither success nor her friends could assuage it. Like a force of nature she blew aside conventions and rode the storm of her passion to the pinnacle of rock and roll. But even on top of the world, she felt she was sitting by herself. Crisscrossing the country, she and thousands like her lived as nomads in an alien world. In Tom Wolfe's words, they were "sailing like gypsies along the service center fringes" of America.

After Janis Joplin overdosed on heroin at the age of twenty-seven, a close friend described her as the "best publicized homeless person of the sixties."

Dying that same year, 1970, was Bertrand Russell, who at first sight appears less like Janis Joplin than anyone. Lord Russell—the English Voltaire, Cambridge educated, child of privilege, renowned philosopher and mathematician—lived ninety-eight full years, rather than a short twenty-seven, and was famous for his aquiline, patrician profile and diamond-sharp intellect. No one, it seemed, lived a life more rational, more calmly chiseled by the dictates of the mind.

"I like mathematics," he once wrote, "because it is *not* human and has nothing particular to do with this planet or with the whole accidental universe—because, like Spinoza's God, it won't love us in return." Russell's powers of analysis were so formidable that one friend called him "The Day of Judgment." Russell wrote to another, "I feel myself so rugged and ruthless, and somewhat removed from the whole aesthetic side of life—a sort of logic machine warranted to destroy any idea that is not very robust."

Was this the whole story? Far from it. Orphaned at the age of three by the death of his parents, and orphaned philosophically at the age of sixteen by his atheism, Russell was no logic machine. He was literally ravenous for home, for love, and for children of his own. All his life he was torn—torn between his parents and his grandparents, between his atheism and his mysticism, between his four wives and his many mistresses, between his life of scholarship and his life of public activism, and above all between his keenly analytical mind and his wildly passionate heart.

"He seemed detached in mind and body," one mistress wrote, "but all the furies of hell raged in his eyes." Or as Russell wrote to Lady Ottoline Morrell, another mistress and his deepest love: "The root of the whole thing is loneliness. I have a kind of physical loneliness, which almost anybody can more or less relieve, but which would be only fully relieved by a wife & children. Beyond that, I have a very internal & terrible spiritual loneliness.... I have dreamed of a combination of spiritual & physical companionship, and if I had the good fortune to find it, I could have become something better than I shall ever be."

Companionship, love, home, and the search for purpose and fulfillment in life—for all their differences, Janis Joplin and Bertrand Russell speak for us all. Our deepest human yearning is to know a sense of meaning and belonging in this journey that is our life.

Have you felt that longing?

LIFE AS A JOURNEY

As far back as there have been human beings, there have been stories. From the bard weaving word magic around the fire, to the troubadour singing in the great hall, to the celluloid myths of the grand Hollywood mythmakers, nothing is more human than stories and storytelling. And no stories are more resonant than those that tap the deepest reservoirs of what it is to be human. But one theme is almost universal—the picture of life as a journey.

"Midway on our life's journey I found myself in a dark wood." So begins Dante's famous metaphysical adventure story, *Divine Comedy*. Life as journey—from the Hebrew book of *Exodus* to Homer's *Odyssey*, Virgil's *Aeneid*, Geoffrey Chaucer's *Canterbury Tales*, Miguel de Cervantes's *Don Quixote*, John Bunyan's *Pilgrim's Progress*, Mark Twain's *Huckleberry Finn*, Joseph Conrad's *Heart of Darkness*, Hermann Hesse's *Siddhartha*, Jack Kerouac's *On the Road*—the examples go on and on, and these are only Western ones. The picture is everywhere in every century. Life is a journey, a voyage, a quest, a pilgrimage, a personal odyssey, and we're all at some unknown point between the beginning and the end of it.

Dictionaries tell us that an odyssey is a long wandering marked by many changes of fortune. The word, of course, comes to us from Homer and the epic age of Greece. But it aptly connotes the progress and setbacks, the twists and turns, the ups and downs of our human experience. "The soul is an exile and a wanderer," Plutarch wrote, following Plato.

"Midway on our life's journey," Dante had written. He was then thirty-five, at what turned out to be the exact halfway point in a life that lasted precisely the biblical "three score years and ten." If our human lot is to journey that long—give or take a few years—at some point we ask, What will they all add up to? Where have we come from? Where are we going?

Usually we raise such questions in the idealism of our youth, only to have them shouldered aside by the busy importance of midlife, then gradually cowed into silence by the tolling bell of our mortality—in deepening wrinkles, graying hair, shortening breath, thickening waistlines, and more of our sentences beginning "In my day..."

War, sickness, accident, or natural disaster can always break in early, of course. But not for most. Most of us feel immortal in our teens and twenties, then move through life so fast in our thirties and forties that we lose sight of the journey and think only of our careers. Even in our fifties we barely hear the roar of the rapids several bends down the river.

Part of the conceit of the modern age is that we can arrest the flow of time with our science and technology. But time and death remain unstoppable. For some the end comes before they've even begun to think. For others the shock of realization is a bracing, just-in-time reminder. Lee Iacocca, the legendary carmaker, wrote in his autobiography: "Here I am in the twilight years of my life, still wondering what it's all about.... I can tell you this, fame and fortune is for the birds."

MAKING SENSE OF A SHORT STAY

Journeying and movement are bigger themes than ever in the twentieth and twenty-first centuries, when travel has become so central that ours is literally a world on the move. The restless journeying in the past of pilgrims, explorers, conquerors, and colonizers has been overshadowed by the restlessness of modern nomads such as immigrants and exiles, businesspeople and tourists. For one reason or another, more and more people have been uprooted and made to feel at home nowhere. But the deepest meaning of journeying is still the oldest one—the sense that the journey is the best metaphor for life itself.

"What is life," George Santayana asked, "but a form of motion and a journey through a foreign world?"

In his famous speech "My Credo," delivered in Berlin in 1932, Albert Einstein put it this way: "Our situation on this earth seems strange. Everyone of us appears here involuntarily and uninvited for a short stay, without knowing the whys and the wherefore."

For journalist Malcolm Muggeridge, this theme became the motif for his entire life. "The first thing I remember about the world—and I pray it may be the last—is that I was a stranger in it. This feeling, which everyone has in some degree, and which is at once the glory and desolation of *homo sapiens,* provides the only thread of consistency that I can see in my life."

Actress Jessica Lange felt the same. "The main thing that I sensed back in my childhood," she said, "was this inescapable yearning that I could never satisfy. Even now at times I experience an inescapable loneliness and isolation.... Oh, God, how I remember that feeling, though. Sitting on the front steps on a summer night and hearing a lawn mower in the distance and a screen door slamming somewhere. It would actually make my heart *ache.*"

One day, a few years ago, I suddenly woke up again to this live sense of journey. Facing the prospect of a suspected brain tumor, I was in a hospital in northern Virginia ready to undergo a brain scan. A nurse entered the room briskly and said, "Excuse my asking, but are you claustrophobic?"

"No," I answered.

"Good," she said. "Some people can't take the scanner. Our nickname for it is the 'coffin machine.'"

"Thanks very much," I replied lightly.

Five minutes later it was hard to get her words out of my mind. Both that session and the next turned out to be an unexpected time of personal review. Just as a drowning person sees his life flash before his eyes, so I saw the years of my life scroll across my mind as I lay in my "coffin."

I was born in China during World War II, grew up in the midst of a terrible famine and plague in which millions—including my two brothers—died, and lived to witness the reign of terror that climaxed the revolution of Mao Zedong. Since then I've lived on three continents and in a score of cities. Movement and uprootedness have been a staple of my life. And in the coffin machine, the memories of that life came to me not like an archaic black-and-white documentary but as reality. Each memory was alive with sights and sounds and smells. I shivered at the still-unrealized potential of hopes, dreams, and fears.

It was during that extraordinary life-review that I felt again what I first felt in my twenties—the wonder of this brief but glorious journey of life. As Winston Churchill said in the last days of his life, "It has been a grand journey—well worth making once." I, too, saw vividly the sense I had made of this journey since my youth. And I thought of many I know who seek now to make sense of their lives as a journey.

This book comes from that experience. Written for those who care and those who are open, it's a seeker's road map to the quest for meaning. It charts the road toward meaning taken by countless thoughtful seekers over the centuries and shows how it can be found today.

To be sure, I argue for some choices, not others, and challenge readers to choose a definite path rather than the vacuousness of a perpetually open mind. But the road, the choices, and the thinking are set out openly. The invitation here is to "come and see." It assumes no faith in the reader, only the recognition that the humanness of life as a journey is something we should all care about enough to seek to make sense of it and to make up our minds for ourselves.

———

Have you awakened to the journey of life? Or are you among those drifting down the years? Are you among those so caught up in the project of themselves that they choose not to hear the flow of time? Are you open to care, to think, to seek?

Let your mind and your heart run deep. Come, join the seeker's path on the long journey home.

CHAPTER TWO

AN EXAMINED LIFE IN
AN UNEXAMINING AGE

Several years ago I spoke at a conference near London where the other speaker was E. F. Schumacher, noted economist and author of *Small Is Beautiful.* He began his talk with the story of a recent visit to St. Petersburg, Russia, which in those days of the Soviet era was still under drab communist wraps as Leningrad.

Despite having a map in hand, which he was following painstakingly, Schumacher realized he was lost. What he saw on paper didn't fit what was right before his eyes—several huge Russian Orthodox churches, unmistakable with their golden onion domes. They weren't on the map, yet he was certain he knew which street he was on.

"Ah," said an Intourist guide, trying to be helpful. "That's simple. We don't show churches on our maps."

"It then occurred to me," Schumacher said (and later wrote in *Guide for the Perplexed*), "that this is not the first time I had been given a map which failed to show many things I could see right in front of my eyes. All through school and university I had been given maps of life and knowledge on which there was hardly a trace of many of the things that I most cared about and that seemed to me to be of the greatest possible importance to the conduct of my life." In short, he said, the mental maps with which he was supplied as a European intellectual gave no place to the faith that was so vital to him.

MISTAKEN MAPMAKERS

The observation by Socrates in his trial that "the unexamined life is not worth living" may be the most famous saying from the classical world—and also the least followed. Today's challenge is to lead an examined life in an unexamining age. The difficulty lies partly in our frantic busyness: Who has time to stop and ask what it's all about and where we're running? But the real problem lies elsewhere. Many people have such poorly detailed mental "maps" to follow—lacking especially in markers toward faith and the spirit—that we don't know *how* to pursue an examined life. What we think we see doesn't match what we're told. Are we not being told everything?

It's as if we're in Aldous Huxley's *Brave New World,* where copies of the Bible and several classics of Western faith, along with certain masterpieces of art and science, have been locked away. These were only "pornographic old books," one character explained, pointing out that "God isn't compatible with machinery and scientific medicine and universal happiness."

In France of the 1940s, Simone Weil lamented, "To find a place in the budget for the eternal is not in the spirit of our age." In America a decade later, Herman Wouk wrote of believing Jews groping in "the modern blackout of religious belief."

Still later, writer Anne Lamott recalled her experience of growing up near San Francisco: "None of the adults in our circle believed. Believing meant that you were stupid. Ignorant people believed, uncouth people believed, and we were heavily couth." Writer Annie Dillard felt obliged to tell the *New York Times Magazine,* "Just because I'm religious doesn't mean I'm insane."

The fact is that many of the greatest thinkers, writers, artists, musicians, scientists, inventors, poets, and reformers throughout Western history have been people of profound and genuine faith— Augustine, Dante, Gutenberg, Pascal, Rembrandt, Newton, Bach, Handel, Wilberforce, Dostoevsky, and T. S. Eliot, to name a few—yet faith continues to be dismissed by many of the educated and cultured as something only for the uneducated and uncultured.

Another fact is that almost all great reforms in Western history— including the banning of infanticide, the abolition of slavery, the rise of the women's movement, and progress in civil rights—have been inspired by faith and led by people of faith. Yet faith itself is commonly dismissed as reactionary.

Still another fact is that secular ideologies, not religion, proved responsible in the last century for the Holocaust, the Gulag, and the killing fields. And that religion, not secular philosophies, was influential in provoking the worldwide thrust for freedom and democracy in the last several decades.

Yet Western culture's acknowledged leaders and influencers still persist in making and using "maps" that ignore faith and spirituality. Any serious mention of faith in many spheres of public life is considered intrusive, undemocratic, quite out of place—even when the majority of people understand themselves and their lives, public as well as private, from the perspective of their faith. This seems particularly true in the United States, which social scientist Peter L. Berger described as "a nation of Indians ruled by Swedes"—Americans are as religious as people in India, the world's most religious country, yet significant sectors of American leadership are more typical of Sweden, one of the most secular of societies.

One historian caught the absurdity when he overheard a Manhattan attorney comment on how religious his fellow Americans are. "Millions of people," the lawyer muttered, "now believe what nobody believes anymore."

TONE-DEAF AND COLOR-BLIND

On our culture's leading edge, disregard for faith springs partially from open hostility to it. Voltaire's notorious contempt for religion— "Crush the infamous thing!"—will probably be echoed in every generation, as in media mogul Ted Turner's dismissal of the Christian faith as "a religion for losers."

But the wider and deeper problem is not so much animosity as what has been termed tone deafness. In Max Weber's apt description, too many of today's thinking people are "unmusical." They're unable to hear or appreciate the score by which most of their fellow human beings orchestrate their lives. But it's "an acoustical illusion," Friedrich Nietzsche realized, "that where nothing is heard there *is* nothing." As an Orthodox Jew, novelist Herman Wouk protested that agnosticism, "when it becomes an ear-stopping dogma, may be as bad a mental handicap as superstition."

Or we could think of the impairment as one of sight. From Germany in the 1930s, Albert Einstein wrote that a religious sense of the mysterious is the "most beautiful and deepest experience a man can have.... He who never had this experience seems to me, if not dead, then at least blind." Color blindness is the apt metaphor for some: They miss the rich-hued splendor of the spiritual vision of life and see only the colder, duller world of black and white.

Early in Charles Darwin's life, his first visit to the Brazilian rain forest had suffused him with "feelings of wonder, admiration, and devotion." Later, increasingly influenced by the effects of his chosen philosophy of naturalism, he acknowledged that he had lost the faculty for comprehending anything apart from empirical data. "But now the grandest scenes would not cause any such convictions and feelings to rise in my mind. It may be truly said that I am like a man who has become color blind."

Darwin's naturalism affected his feel for all the arts. As he wrote to a friend, "I am glad you were at the 'Messiah,' it is the one thing I should like to hear again, but I dare say I should find my soul too dried up to appreciate it as in old days; and then I should feel very flat, for it is a horrid bore to feel as I constantly do, that I am a withered leaf for every subject except science."

Poetry, drama, art, music—they all used to delight him, Darwin confessed in his autobiography. "But now for many years I cannot endure to read a line of poetry; I have tried recently to read Shakespeare, and found it so intolerably dull that it nauseated me. I have also almost lost my taste for pictures or music.... My mind seems to have become a kind of machine for grinding general laws out of large collections of facts."

AN INVITATION TO TRAVEL

Nevertheless, in the midst of all these failures in apprehending or appreciating faith, fresh thinking is sprouting. The "sea of faith" that Matthew Arnold famously saw receding on Dover Beach is now coming in again. The "waters of religion" that Nietzsche thought were "ebbing away into stagnant pools" are rushing back with life-giving force. Eternal questions and yearnings are thrusting their way up between the cracks in the sterile world of secular disenchantment.

How do we unriddle the mystery of life and make the most of it? What does it mean to find ourselves guests on a tiny, spinning blue ball in a vast universe? Is our sense of individual uniqueness backed by a guarantee, or are we only dust in the wind? What explains our grotesque human capacity for slaughtering our fellow human beings by day and listening to classical music in the evening? Is there an emergency number to call when we have vandalized our planet home like a drunken rock star on a hotel rampage? Why is birth the automatic qualification for death? How should we live, knowing that we each owe death one life, and nothing we can ever do will ransom us? What recourse do we have if we conclude that the world should have been otherwise?

Long Journey Home is written for those who are asking enduring questions like these. It charts the road that beckons a thoughtful person's quest for meaning. In particular it highlights four stages of the journey that countless people have passed through over the centuries. But before we set out, let me make a few things clear so as to avoid both needless fears and exaggerated expectations.

First, the present approach makes no pretense of originality. As Mark Twain pointed out, only Adam could claim to say something new, knowing that nobody had ever said it before. For the rest of us, repeating and restating are the name of the game. When it comes to the journey of life, tradition is a help, however, not a handicap, since today's road less traveled is yesterday's well-beaten path, made all the more assuring by those who've gone before. As T. S. Eliot observed, "Someone said, 'The dead writers are remote from us because we know so much more than they did.' Precisely, and they are that which we know."

Second, the approach taken here—the thoughtful seeker's journey—is not the only way. Nor is it the required way. There are as many paths in the quest for meaning as there are people who join the quest. As a consequence, thoughtful seekers often find themselves to be especially solitary. In thinking circles their path often sets them apart because they're seekers; in other circles it may set them apart because they're thinkers. The combination—seeking and thinking—is what makes them rare.

(Obviously, the thoughtful seeker I have in mind is not to be confused with the much-mocked "intellectual," the person so caught up in the world of ideas that he or she has lost touch with ordinary life. Although such a person is "very clever," Margot Asquith noted, "sometimes his brains go to his head." The intellectual, as Dwight Eisenhower quipped, is "a man who takes more words than necessary to tell us more than he knows.")

Third, the present approach will not attempt to set out "proofs" but rather to indicate the paths and pointers that, if followed, will lead to sure convictions. The notion of proof has an exaggerated status in our age. As heirs and beneficiaries of science, we accord a profound respect to verification and exactitude, but science and mathematics are the farthest things from our minds when we pause to appreciate a sunset, fall in love, or come to faith in God.

The reason is that strict mathematical and scientific proofs have to do with lower areas of life, while falling in love and coming to faith are higher, more important matters—not because they're less rational, but because they're more personal. They engage the whole person rather than the mind alone. As G. K. Chesterton noted with forgivable exaggeration, we "are all exact and scientific on the subjects we do not care about." The quest for meaning isn't so much a mathematician's proof as a matchmaker's proposal, as philosopher Peter Kreeft reminds us.

To win consent, the matchmaker's proposal may need to be expressed either simply or profoundly, depending on the seeker. The wording can be shallow enough for a child to paddle in, deep enough for an elephant to swim in, or somewhere in between. For some, a sentence is enough. Asked by a fellow management expert why he had come to faith, Peter Drucker replied, "It's the best deal!" For others, more is required, sufficient to stimulate the wrestling that leads to mature conviction.

Fourth, the present approach is not a demonstration for spectators but an invitation to participants. If the seeker is more than a disembodied mind, if the search is more than strict proofs, then the journey cannot be something merely "thought about." It must be undertaken, beginning with the effort of actually setting out—not reading travel brochures or daydreaming about destinations, but the real travel of living with all the discomforts and dangers.

Spectating will not do. It takes the forward movement of deliberate, dynamic living to make this journey—especially the longest and most important journey of all, the journey from our heads to our hearts and from our hearts to our wills. If the journey is life, then only through living will truths gain force that are otherwise barren platitudes.

That's why the quest is so challenging and why the argument in this book is necessarily incomplete: Each seeker must complete it on his own. For when all is said and done, life's journey isn't about humanity in general, or even the person next door. It's about you and me. Our individual lives are the focus, a picture framed by our birth and death. Our personal goals and principles are under scrutiny; our personal success or failure is in the balance.

And the answers along the way that help us most will not be something new we didn't know before (and probably don't need now), but something that gives expression to the truths already inside ourselves, truths we struggle to grasp in the thick of everyday living. "Ultimately no one can extract from things, books included, more than he already knows," Nietzsche wrote. "What one has no access to through experience, one has no ear for."

BEYOND BOOKS

"Neither Christ nor Buddha nor Socrates wrote a book," noted the Irish poet W. B. Yeats, "for to do that is to exchange life for a logical process." What you're reading now is a book, but a book that points to a path beyond books, the path of vigorous thought and living.

"He who sees me sees the teaching," said the Buddha to those who gathered around him.

"We teach ourselves; Zen merely points the way," say its advocates.

"Taste and see," cried the Hebrew psalmist to his listeners.

"Follow me," said Jesus of Nazareth to his disciples.

All the leaders of the world's great faiths have agreed on one thing: The seeker's quest for meaning will never be fulfilled by reading and reflection alone. The invitation is to *set out*.

———

Are you leading an examined life? Or are you living in the hand-me-down ideas of others? Do you pick up the music coming from dimensions beyond the here and now? Or are you one of those who just don't get it?

Let your mind and your heart run deep. Come, join the seeker's path on the long journey home.

PART ONE

A TIME FOR QUESTIONS

CHAPTER THREE

A WORLD OF
DIFFERENCE

Fatuous, preposterous, desultory—Malcolm Muggeridge was famous for the way he rolled favorite words around his mouth, savoring each one like a gourmand relishing a mouthful, before delivering them in his incomparable way of speaking. Behind the rich currency of his speech was not just a love of language but a life rich in experiencing the things of which he spoke. He therefore took seriously only the solid and the proven. All else, including much that others considered solid, he had already weighed and found wanting—fatuous, preposterous, and desultory, in fact, compared with the rocklike realities he sought.

One of the milestone experiences in Muggeridge's life was his celebrated suicide attempt in Africa in 1943, recounted in his memoirs, *Chronicles of Wasted Time.* He was forty years old, and those four decades had been a schooling in progressive disillusionment. He described his four years at Cambridge University as "the most futile and dismal of my whole life." Three years in India, perhaps the most religious country in the world, shattered his early religious beliefs. Two years in Stalin's Russia, to which he had gone as a fervent, utopian socialist, left his idealistic materialism in ruins. (Muggeridge's was the first voice to report and denounce the horrors of Stalin's induced famine of 1932–33 that starved to death more than four million people.) The 1930s as a whole he summed up as "a decade which began with the illusion of progress without tears and ended in the reality of tears without progress."

Even World War II, with all its demands for sacrifice and heroism, seemed to offer Muggeridge no chance of redemption. He was turned down on his first attempt to enlist, and on finally being accepted as a spy in the British Secret Service, found himself far from the glamorous action depicted in espionage novels. He was stuck in Lourenço Marques, Mozambique, monitoring the German disruption of Allied shipping. Bored, listless, and desolate, he wrote home to his wife, Kitty, in March 1943, "Much of the time I spend wishing I was dead, wondering why I am doing what I have to do, putting up my own faint struggle with the tedium of time."

One night, as Muggeridge wrote later, "the absurdity, the futility, the degradation" struck home. "I lay on my bed full of stale liquor and despair; alone in the house, and, as it seemed, utterly alone, not just in Lourenço Marques, in Africa, in the world. Alone in the universe, in eternity. With no glimmer of light in the prevailing blackness; no human voice I could hope to hear, or human heart I could hope to reach; no God to whom I could turn, or Saviour to take my hand." Cheated by his position of war's only solace—death—"it came into my mind that there was, after all, one death I could still procure. My own. I decided to kill myself."

Choosing to do so by drowning, Muggeridge drove six miles out of town, undressed, left his clothes on the beach, waded out in the dark cold water, and started swimming. It felt easy. It was settled.

Quickly he was out of sight of the beach and could see only the lights from the distant town. But all of a sudden he began to tremble, and then, without thinking or deciding, he began to swim back to shore, his eyes fixed on the glow from Peter's Café and the Costa da Sol. "They were lights of the world; they were the lights of my home, my habitat, where I belonged. I must reach them. There followed an overwhelming joy such as I had never experienced before; an ecstasy."

Was Muggeridge describing his conversion, a Damascus Road experience in the ocean off Mozambique? Not at all, but he later saw it was a turning point, a forward thrust in his long search. "Though I scarcely realized it at the time and subsequently only very slowly and dimly, this episode represented for me one of those deep changes which take place in our lives…. Whereby, thenceforth, all my values and pursuits and hopes were going to undergo a total transformation." In words that echo Plato's parable of the cave, Muggeridge wrote, "In a tiny dungeon of the ego, chained and manacled, I had glimpsed a glimmer of light coming through a barred window high above me." Having seen that glimmer, he was now absorbed with the quest to understand it. What Muggeridge had acted on suddenly and intuitively—a bid for life and purpose—he had to find a reason for.

THE MOMENT THAT MAKES THE SEEKER

No one could be less conventional and predictable than Malcolm Muggeridge. But his experience exemplifies the first stage in every seeker's journey—a time for questions. We become aware of a sense of reaching out that forces us to ask where we are in life. We must find meaning beyond the meaning we know.

The term "seeker" is in vogue today but used far too casually. Often it's only a synonym for the spiritually unattached: Seekers are those who do *not* identify themselves as Christian, Jew, Muslim, Buddhist, atheist, or whatever, or who do *not* attend or belong to any church, synagogue, mosque, or meeting place.

Such seekers are rarely looking for anything in particular. Often they're drifters, little different from the hoppers and shoppers who surf the media and cruise the malls. Cool, noncommittal, ever-open, concerned only to cover all bases, they're eternally ready to be converted and reconverted ad nauseam. They're like a character Anita Brookner described in her novel *Altered States:* "Her life was an improvisation, without roots, without commitments, without guarantees."

True seekers are quite different. On meeting them you feel their seriousness, their driven restlessness. Something in life has awakened questions—perhaps something positive, like a sense of awe in the face of beauty; perhaps something negative, like a crisis or a collapsed confidence. They have been forced to reconsider. They must find answers outside their present answers.

Seekers are people for whom life, or a part of life, has become a point of wonder, a question, a problem, an irritation. It happens so intensely, so persistently, that a sense of need consumes them and launches them on their quest.

An immediate caution: The "sense of need" does not in itself justify or guarantee a new belief. People do not come to believe in the answers they seek because of need. That would be irrational and make them vulnerable to the accusation that faith is a projection and a crutch. Rather, seekers *dis*believe what they believed before because of new questions their previous beliefs couldn't answer. Conceivably, they may seek and seek and never find a new belief, then either despair or come to the conclusion that the search itself is its only reward. Muggeridge himself, as one biographer commented, "knew what he disbelieved long before he knew what he believed."

For some people in this initial stage of seeking, the questions can be dramatic and intense. In his *Confession* Leo Tolstoy traced the start of his search for meaning to the double-jolt of the death of his brother Nicholas and the sight of a guillotine. The same two things, a public execution and the death of a brother, were instrumental in Fyodor Dostoevsky's awakening.

Centuries earlier, Augustine of Hippo in his *Confessions* expressed an anguished questioning with vivid intensity: "I carried about me a cut and bleeding soul, that could not bear to be carried by me, and where I could put it, I could not discover. Not in pleasant groves, not in games and singing, nor in the fragrant corners of a garden. Not in the company of a dinner table, not in the delights of the bed: not even in my books and poetry. It floundered in a void and fell back on me. I remained a haunted spot, which gave me no rest, from which I could not escape. For where could my heart flee from my heart? Where could I escape myself? Where would I not dog my own footsteps?"

For others, the questions may surface more quietly. At the funeral of his father, management consultant Charles Handy suddenly realized how this modest man had affected the lives of hundreds in ways he had never imagined. "I realized that what one believes about life, and the point of life, does matter. I had put my faith, until that moment, in success, money, and family, probably in that order. I still think these things are important, although I would now reverse the order, but I hanker after a bigger frame in which to put them."

Whether quiet or dramatic, the eruption of questions is decisive. Zen Buddhism teaches that the key to inner growth is "a red-hot coal stuck in the throat"—an obstacle so deep that we can't swallow it and can't cough it up. A grain of sand in the pearl, a burr under the saddle, a haunting dream, a wordless intuition that there must be "something more"—the pictures vary, but the experiences point in the same direction: Suddenly life can no longer be taken for granted. A thrusting question has punctured the complacency, bursting the adequacy of some previous source of meaning.

A seeker is born.

THE ANIMAL THAT ASKS AND ASKS

Inevitably, the true seeker's questions bore into the essence of our existence.

Unique among living species, human life is aware of itself, yet we find ourselves in a world that doesn't explain itself. So we're impelled to ask why things are as they are and how we fit in. What gives life to life? Why is there something rather than nothing? Deep inside us we know the facts of the matter are not the end of the matter. So we seek a final explanation, a source of meaning that goes as far back as one can go, an ultimate answer before which all questions cease.

This will to find meaning is fundamental. It is "the primary motivational force in man," according to psychiatrist Viktor Frankl. "Meaning is not a luxury for us," says philosopher Dallas Willard. "It is a kind of spiritual oxygen, we might say, that enables our souls to live." Abraham Heschel expressed it from his Jewish viewpoint: "It is not enough for me to be able to say 'I am'; I want to know *who I am* and in relation to whom I live. It is not enough for me to ask questions; I want to know how to answer the one question that seems to encompass everything I face: What am I here for?"

Immanuel Kant, greatest of the Enlightenment philosophers, summarized the four big questions of life around which we circle: "What can we know? What must we do? What can we hope for? What is man?" The French postimpressionist painter Paul Gauguin portrayed them as three: "Where do we come from? What are we? Where are we going?" Literary critic George Steiner says simply, "More than *homo sapiens,* we are *homo quaerens,* the animal that asks and asks."

To help us handle such questions, we all have a philosophy or vision of life, a "world-view," whether we're aware of it or not. It's the story line or road map or lens with which we interpret all our experience of life. It determines how we see reality and our own identity and how we decide issues of morality.

Most of the time our world-views are unconscious, but even when we don't see them, we see *by* them. "The truly powerful ideas," Dallas Willard points out, "are precisely the ones that do not have to justify themselves." World-views are thus much deeper than such self-conscious philosophies as Marxism and existentialism.

We derive our world-views from a variety of sources—parents, education, cultural background, experiences, and discoveries. Some people—humanists, for example—are quite candid that these beliefs are their own invention. Others, such as Jews, Christians, and Muslims, claim that their world-views have been disclosed from outside human experience, through a form of revelation.

But for all their differences, our ways of viewing life are fundamental and necessary to each of us because they provide a sense of meaning and belonging. They help us make sense of our lives and find security in our worlds. They're a world within the world, and they make a world of difference.

NOTE WHAT THEY DO, NOT WHAT THEY SAY

What the seeker seeks is meaning. Yet it has recently been fashionable in educated circles to sneer at such a search. Even worse has been the contempt for any supposed success in the pursuit, as if meaning was only deception and the possession of it a numbing illusion. "Take away the life-lie from the average man and you take away his happiness," said Henrik Ibsen, the Norwegian playwright.

Such cynics need not deter a seeker. We should note what they do, not what they say, for even the claim that life is meaningless is an assertion of meaning. As we shall see many times as we survey this journey, any argument is arguable, and no arguments are unarguable, but there are thoughts that can be thought and not lived. Moreover, those who are cynical about life's meaning often live lives rich with substance and significance.

"We are here on earth to fart about," novelist Kurt Vonnegut said. "Don't let anyone tell you different." But his many books and the passionate intensity of even his descriptions of absurdity tell another story.

Alfred Nobel wrote a famous "police blotter" self-description: "Alfred Nobel—pitiful creature, ought to have been suffocated by a humane physician when he made his howling entrance into this life.... Important events in his life: none." Near his death he wrote, "How pitiful to strive to be someone or something in the motley crowd of 1.4 billion two-legged, tailless apes whining around on our revolving earth projectile." But Nobel's life and the celebrated prizes named after him demonstrate beyond doubt that he did strive to be someone. Far closer to his real views were other words he had written, read by a friend at his funeral: "Silent you stand before the altar of death! Life here and life after constitute an eternal conundrum; but its expiring spark awakens us to holy devotion and quiets every other voice except that of religion. Eternity has the floor."

WORTH THE TROUBLE?

Plato advised that each person take the best human theory "and let this be the raft on which one sails through life—not without risk, as I admit, if one cannot find some word of God which will surely and safely carry him." Is such a voyage worth the risk?

"There is only one really serious philosophical problem," wrote Albert Camus in the opening words of *The Myth of Sisyphus,* "that of suicide. To judge that life is or is not worth the trouble of being lived, this is to reply to the fundamental question of philosophy."

In swimming out into the black night of the ocean off Mozambique, Muggeridge knew his disillusionment with all he had trusted till that moment. But in trembling, in turning around, in striking out for the distant shore and the faraway lights, he contradicted that despair. Far from claiming to find or believe anything at that moment, he had become a seeker. From then on, for all its lurches and detours, his life was a quest to discover why life was worth the trouble.

———

Are you open to the full interrogation of life? Or are you closed to the search because you believe what you've always believed without question? Have you pondered the logic of your experiences and dared to follow the direction of their limits and promptings?

Let your heart and mind run deep. Come farther down the seeker's path on the long journey home.

CHAPTER FOUR

TRADING OUR
TOMORROWS

Night had fallen on Death Valley, but for the three men sitting there on the edge of a cliff in the spring of 1975, the darkness was anything but inert. It was crackling with anticipation and with the electronic music of Karlheinz Stockhausen's *Kontakte*.

Soon, for each of them in different ways, it was also exploding with the ecstatic visions of their LSD tripping. Two of them, the younger Americans, had experienced acid before. For the third, a Frenchman in his late forties, the experience was novel and shattering. Two hours later he gestured toward the starry heavens: "The sky has exploded," he cried, "and the stars are raining down on me. I know this is not true, but it is the Truth."

The trip was enough of a gamble for the Americans. It was their idea, and they might have blown the fuses of the man they considered "the master thinker of our era." It was a far greater risk for Michel Foucault, world-famous philosopher, militant, and professor at the prestigious Collège de France, but one he undertook eagerly.

Ever since he was a young man, Foucault had been on the Nietzschean quest "to become what one is," or as Nietzsche had expressed it more strangely: "Why am I alive? What lesson am I to learn from life? How did I become what I am and why do I suffer from being what I am?" Foucault aimed to complete his quest through the ordeal of "limit experiences" (experiencing extremes in order to unleash creative forces and intense joy) and through the rediscovery of the "Dionysian element" in his personality (the wild, untamed animal energy within).

"It is forbidden to forbid," the notorious Sorbonne slogan had protested in 1968, reflecting Foucault's thought. That night in Death Valley he increased the stakes of his lifelong wager. He had always been fascinated with madness, violence, perversion, suicide, and death; now he wanted to liberate himself further by transgressing all boundaries.

Buffeted by a strong wind, the three men huddled together on the promontory. Foucault spoke again, tears streaming down his face: "I am very happy. Tonight I achieved a full perspective on myself. I now understand my sexuality. We must go home again."

Only Foucault's friends know the full story of that evening in Death Valley, but there's no question that it changed him—especially his thinking on sexuality. It propelled him with reckless abandon into the doomed, midseventies San Francisco world of free sex, powerful acid, altered states of consciousness, and death from AIDS. Defiant in its openness, reckless in its conviviality, the homosexual world of Castro, Polk, and Folsom Streets had suddenly become one of the wildest, least inhibited sexual communities in history. For Michel Foucault, the lure was irresistible. Here was a nonstop testing ground rich in "limit experiences" for both body and mind.

To be fair, the dreaded term AIDS wasn't in currency in the seventies and was unknown to most people until film star Rock Hudson died of it in August 1984, just two months after Foucault himself. But the character and consequences of "the gay cancer" were slowly becoming undeniable, and Foucault faced the gamble openly.

"Should I take chances with my life?" a California student asked Foucault one day.

"By all means! Take risks, go out on a limb!" Foucault replied.

"But I yearn for solutions."

"There are no solutions," he said.

"Then at least some answers."

"There are no answers!" the philosopher exclaimed.

A LOST WAGER

Foucault gradually came to associate death with pleasure, especially after surviving a brush with death back home in Paris. In a 1982 interview he said, "I would like and hope I'll die of an overdose of pleasure of any kind." Asked to explain, he added: "Because I think that the kind of pleasure I would consider as *the* real pleasure would be so deep, so intense, so overwhelming that I couldn't survive it. I would die." He used to say, quoting Nietzsche's *Beyond Good and Evil,* "It may be a basic characteristic of existence that those who know it completely would perish."

In *The History of Sexuality,* Foucault wrote, "The Faustian pact, whose temptation has been instilled in us by the deployment of sexuality, is now as follows: to exchange life in its entirety for sex itself, for the truth and sovereignty of sex. Sex is worth dying for."

In the end, the character of his Faustian pact was unmistakable: "To die for the love of boys," he said. "What could be more beautiful?" There was, he believed, no more fitting climax to his work than the free embrace of a beautiful death. Was he courting AIDS and committing suicide? No, said his friends. In those last months before the dark plague came into the full light of day, Foucault and his partners wagered their lives and simply lost the wager.

"If I know the truth," Foucault had said in a revealing interview, "I will be changed. And maybe I will be saved. Or maybe I'll die, but I think that is the same for me anyway."

Truth Twisters with a Reason

The story of Michel Foucault's dark wager of death-for-pleasure opens up an important question for anyone exploring the quest for meaning. If it's so important to have a world-view, a philosophy of life, a set of governing beliefs, why aren't we conscious of it more often? Why don't people care more about it? Why do most people not seem to mind the "unexamined life" that Socrates thought was not worth living?

One obvious answer is that a dependable world-view is like good health. It's usually experienced most when it's talked about least. In the same way, philosophies of life that work well are those of which we're barely aware, like a pair of glasses we don't notice until they're dirty or scratched. We think *with* our world-view, not about it.

Another obvious answer is that many people are only too happy to leave such questions to others, especially to those whom society considers designated experts, such as priests, pundits, or psychologists.

But there's a deeper answer still. As many thinkers over the centuries have observed, human beings need a source of meaning and belonging, yet we also mount defenses against thinking and caring too deeply about the human condition—and especially against the fact that we all will die.

"All but Death, can be Adjusted," wrote Emily Dickinson. "Any man who says he is not afraid of death is a liar," said Winston Churchill. The reason is obvious. Death is the fear behind all other fears, the endmost end beyond which there is no beginning. For all our limitless mental reach, our minds and imaginations are cased in finite, transient bodies. One moment we see a cloudless forever; the next we hear a rasping death rattle. Being human we know this, and being human we can do nothing about it.

The Swiss sculptor Alberto Giacometti knew well the absolute claim of time and death. When he reached thirty, he created *No More Play*, a sculpture portraying a field of graves and a meditation on the theme of death. When asked why he was a sculptor, he would often reply, "So as not to die." Yet nearing his end, he said: "I am convinced that nobody in the world believes he must die. Only an instant before death, he doesn't believe in it. How could he? He lives, which is fact, and everything in him lives, and still a fraction of a second before death he lives, and in no way can he be conscious of death."

So yes, we're "truth seekers," but that isn't the whole story. We're also "truth twisters." Sometimes truth is a matter of a serious search; sometimes it's an intellectual game—played for a reason. "We all fear truth," Nietzsche wrote in *Ecce Homo*. "Humankind," as T. S. Eliot observed, "cannot bear very much reality." There's a threat in the trio of reality, time, and death that we instinctively seek to deny.

TRADING AWAY TOMORROW

Bargaining is one of our two most common forms of denial. Bargaining is our strategy for seeking to gain what we most want in life by trying to strike a bargain with death (or God or the devil). We sell our very souls for the sake of more power, more knowledge, more experience, more pleasure, or more time. In the words of the Kris Kristofferson song made famous by Janis Joplin, we try to trade all our tomorrows "for one single yesterday."

As Foucault's story shows, talk of bargaining inevitably conjures up the image of Dr. Faust. Sometimes traced to Simon Magus in the New Testament, the Faust figure is based on a shadowy German necromancer in the sixteenth century. But whether in poetry, drama, novels, or opera—as envisioned by Christopher Marlowe or Goethe or Berlioz or Honoré de Balzac or Oscar Wilde or Thomas Mann—the picture is of the restless insatiable striver, not just curious but lusting to know, to experience, to possess.

On one hand, the Faustian drive always includes something admirable—the daring human reach, stretching to its limits. Knowledge and experience are pressed higher, farther, faster, beyond all previous bounds. On the other hand, the drive almost always includes something terrible as well. In all the stories of the devil's bargains one point is clear: The devil is a reliable businessman who keeps his side of the deal and insists that we keep ours.

Marlowe's Mephistopheles reminds his victim, "Fools that must laugh on earth will weep in hell." The cryptic saying on Balzac's wild ass's skin is clear from the start: "Possess me and thou shalt possess all things. But thy life is forfeit to me. So hath God willed it. Express a desire and thy desire shall be fulfilled. But let thy wishes be measured against thy life. Here it lies. Every wish will diminish me and diminish thy days. Dost thou desire me? Take, and God will grant thy wish. Amen."

Intriguingly, Goethe's *Faust* was the book Sigmund Freud quoted most often, while Balzac's *The Wild Ass's Skin* was the last thing he chose to read on the day of his death by euthanasia. Bargaining with the devil was obviously much on his mind. It must also have been prominent in the thinking of photographer Robert Mapplethorpe, who made transgression central to his work and pushed his sexually posed subjects beyond their limits by repeating the phrase, "Do it for Satan!" He even wore horns for a famous self-portrait.

None of us is immune to the basic temptation behind such bargaining. What is more human than the desire to wave time aside and more fully enjoy the pleasurable present? We can always attend to reality later. "Give me chastity," Augustine prayed earnestly, "but not yet." Who hasn't wished, perhaps even prayed, to be excused the consequence of some deed just this once? What have we not promised, if only the teacher never sees or our spouse never knows? There's nothing, it seems, we will not vow for tomorrow, if only today we gain a little more time, a little more success, a little more pleasure.

Whether extreme or mild, conscious or unconscious, the impulse to bargain is the same—a futile effort to avoid reality, to slow time, to deny death. Even our addictions are a response to this impulse, as we risk long-term loss for short-term gain, living life as a postponed suicide without ever noticing it.

In the end, all our bargaining proves a waste of time. As Achilles said in *The Iliad* to Lycaon, the Trojan prince: "Fool, don't talk to me of ransom.... Come, friend, you too must die. Why moan about it so?"

Since so many of us are in the business of bargaining, why don't we stop to assess the "bargain" we've gained? "How much land does a man need?" Tolstoy asked in his famous moral fable. His answer was blunt: "Six feet from his head to his heels was all he needed." Tolstoy raised the same issues of the calculus of success that Jesus of Nazareth raised two thousand years ago: "What good is it for someone to gain the whole world, yet forfeit his soul?"

TRANQUILIZED BY THE TRIVIAL

The second common form of denial—our way of ignoring the menacing trio of reality, time, and death—is the human drive toward an entertaining, distracting busyness. Blaise Pascal termed it "diversion"; John Bunyan labeled it "Vanity Fair"; Søren Kierkegaard called it the Philistinism that "tranquilizes itself in the trivial." We shift our attention from what we can do nothing about—death—to what will consume our time and energy and leave no room for serious thinking.

A. E. Housman expressed it this way in "A Shropshire Lad":

> Think no more, lad; laugh, be jolly.
> Why should men make haste to die?
> Empty heads and tongues a-talking
> Make the rough road easy walking,
> And the feather pate of folly
> Bears the falling sky.

The first great exploration of this distractedness was in Blaise Pascal's *Pensées*. Speaking to the leisured world of seventeenth-century France, Pascal discussed such examples of diversion as gambling and hunting (and "why we prefer the hunt to the capture"). "If our condition were truly happy," he declared, "we should not need to divert ourselves from it. Being unable to cure death, wretchedness, and ignorance, men have decided, in order to be happy, not to think about such things. I have often said that the sole cause of man's unhappiness is that he does not know how to stay quietly in his own room."

Since then, our modern world has expanded the array of diversions beyond anything Pascal observed. Modern society itself is one grand diversion—the Republic of Entertainment. With our shops, shows, sports, games, tourism, recreation, cosmetics, plastic surgery, virtual reality, and the endless glorification of health and youth, our culture is a vast conspiracy to make us forget our transience and mortality. We turn away. We tune out. Alibis for reality-escape artists are on every hand. "Modern man is drinking and drugging himself out of awareness," psychologist Ernest Becker wrote, "or he spends his time shopping, which is the same thing."

The drive toward diversion can be seen even in the sharpest minds. In an interview late in his life, Bertrand Russell admitted, "I have to read at least one detective book a day to drug myself against the nuclear threat." In the eighteenth century, David Hume described in his *Treatise of Human Nature* how he shielded himself against the "philosophical melancholy and delirium" brought on by his work as a champion of skepticism: "I drive, I play a game of backgammon, I converse, and am merry with my friends; and when, after three or four hours' amusement, I would return to these speculations, they appear so cold and strained and ridiculous, that I cannot find it in my heart to enter into them further."

WALKING ALONE

Diversion, in the end, works no better than bargaining. Anne Lamott's father called the materialistic frenzy of his hometown "the great tragedy of California, for a life oriented to leisure is in the end a life oriented to death—the greatest leisure of all."

Few of us understand what Emily Dickinson discovered: "To live is so startling, it leaves but little room for other occupations." Instead, most people surround themselves with occupations. They want desperately to be preoccupied. Their deep need is to be tranquilized with the trivial.

All this sets the true seeker quite apart, tragically so. For as novelist Walker Percy noted in *The Moviegoer,* "The search is what anyone would undertake if he were not sunk in the everydayness of his own life." All around are potential seekers who instead are sunk—and who therefore are unlikely to welcome anyone's search when they hear of it. True seekers don't travel in crowds; most often, they wake and walk alone.

———

Does your calculus of success include the bottom line of death, or are you mortgaging your future for the immediate and the short term? Have you been tranquilized by the trivial, or does your sense of life grow from a close attention to reality and time?

Let your mind and heart run deep. Come farther down the seeker's path on the long journey home.

CHAPTER FIVE

GRATEFUL —
BUT WHO DO WE
THANK?

By all accounts, G. K. Chesterton was as colorful in person as he was in his writing. From the flourish of his signature to the sweep of his cape, hat, and sword stick, he was a man in whom life and art, realism and imagination had fused happily to create a figure larger than life but exuberantly real. Not surprisingly, the seed for even his more wildly improbable stories lay in his own experiences. Take, for example, the story of a philosopher and his student that Chesterton included in his book *Manalive*.

Dr. Emerson Eames was the distinguished professor of philosophy and warden of the fictional Brakespeare College, Cambridge. Both a pessimist and an eminent authority on history's most pessimistic thinkers, Eames was a bachelor known for his open-door welcome to friends and favorite students at any hour of day or night.

OUT THE WINDOW

Innocent Smith was one of Eames's brightest undergraduate students. On one particular occasion Smith had spent the best part of the day with the great philosopher, breakfasting on his pessimism at his morning lecture and feasting at different events throughout the day. They finished late at night in the warden's rooms.

"I came to see you at this unearthly hour," Smith had said that morning as they started their ruminations, "because I am coming to the conclusion that existence is really too rotten. I know all the arguments of the thinkers who think otherwise, bishops and agnostics and those sort of people. And knowing you were the greatest living authority on the pessimistic thinkers—"

"All thinkers," Eames said, "are pessimistic thinkers." Beginning with that weary cynicism, he kept up his depressing talk for hour after hour.

Late into the night, something in Innocent Smith finally snapped. He could take no more. "Oh, hang the world!" he cried, slamming his fist on the table.

"Let's give it a bad name first and then hang it," the professor went on unruffled, not really aware that the mood had changed. "A puppy with hydrophobia would probably struggle with life while we killed it, but if we were kind we should kill it. So an omniscient god would put us out of our pain. He would strike us dead."

"Why doesn't he strike us dead?" the student asked.

"He is dead himself," said the philosopher. "That is where he is really enviable. To anyone who thinks, the pleasures of life, trivial and soon tasteless, are bribes to bring us into a torture chamber." The professor was in full flood. Holding a glass of port, he went on, "We all see that for any thinking man mere extinction is the... What are you doing?... Are you mad?... Put that thing down!"

Eames suddenly found himself looking down the cold, small, black barrel of a cocked revolver in the hands of one of his brightest students and most ardent disciples.

"I'll help you out of your hole, old man," Smith said with rough tenderness. "I'll put the puppy out of his pain."

"Do you mean to kill me?" the professor cried, retreating to the window.

"It's not a thing I'd do for everyone," Smith said with emotion. "But you and I seemed to have got so intimate tonight, somehow. I know all your troubles now, and the only cure, old chap.

"It'll soon be over, you know," he continued.

The warden made a run for the window and leaped out awkwardly onto the flying buttress below, where he was trapped. Smith followed to the window and looked down on him like a deeply compassionate benefactor, the revolver in his hand like a gift.

What eventually broke the standoff was not their debate but the dawn. The sun rose slowly, turning the sky from pigeon gray to pink. Bells rang, birds sang, the roofs of the ancient university town were lit with fire, and the sun rose farther with a glory too deep for the skies to hold. Suddenly the unhappy professor on the last morning of his life could bear it no longer.

"Let me come off this place. I can't bear it."

"I rather doubt it will bear you," Smith said, referring to the delicate stonework. "But before you break your neck or I blow out your brains...I want the metaphysical point cleared up. Do I understand that you want to get back to life?"

"I'd give anything to get back," replied the unhappy professor.

"Give anything?" cried Smith. "Then blast your impudence, give us a song!" The startled professor launched into a hymn of gratitude for existence. Satisfied, Smith fired two barrels over his head and let him climb to the ground.

The incident concluded with Innocent Smith explaining the method in his madness.

"Oh, don't you understand, don't you understand?" Smith cried. "I had to do it, Eames. I had to prove you wrong or die. When a man's young he nearly always has someone whom he thinks the top watermark of the mind of man.... Well, you were that to me.... Don't you see that I *had* to prove you really didn't mean it? Or else drown myself in the canal."

Smith continued, "The thing I saw shining in your eyes when you dangled from the buttress was enjoyment at life and not the 'Will to Live.' What you knew when you sat on that damned gargoyle was that the world, when all is said and done, is a wonderful and beautiful place; I know it, because I knew it at the same moment."

HOLES TORN IN LIFE

This superbly told story, far from a pure flight of imagination, is the fruit of the author's own experience. In 1892 Gilbert Keith Chesterton had entered the Slade School of Art in London as an eighteen-year-old student. The end-of-the-century world of art was swirling with decadence and cynicism. A pessimism he called "the black creed" and "starless nihilism" was the rage, and Chesterton himself was drawn to the macabre and the occult.

But one thing held him back—what he described later as a "thin thread of thanks," a sort of "mystical minimum of gratitude." Bursting with gratitude for the gift of life, he woke up to wonder. He then set out to search for a philosophy of life that would allow him to be deeply realistic and yet "enjoy enjoyment" too.

More specifically, he was startled by the simple wonder of the existence of ordinary things, such as a common dandelion. Thinking it over, he noted that "even mere existence, reduced to its mere primary limits, was extraordinary enough to be exciting. Anything was magnificent compared with nothing."

Chesterton's story raises the point that in the quest for meaning, the important thing is not the distinction between "believers" and "unbelievers"; the vital divide is between those who care enough to think seriously about life and those who are indifferent. But what are the sorts of experiences and events that jolt us out of complacency, unmask our most successful diversions, and expose the folly of our most determined efforts at bargaining?

One common way is through the passages of life, such as the openness to questioning in the years between eighteen and twenty-five. Another is through the grand movements of history, such as the unmasking of Marxism through the revelation of the Gulag and the collapse of the Soviet Union. But for thoughtful seekers, perhaps the most important type of triggering experience is what sculptor Alberto Giacometti called "a hole torn in life." When he was nineteen, Giacometti was shocked by the death of an older friend, an experience that obsessed him constantly for a year. For the next twenty-five years it became a point of reference for his tireless, searching mind and a key factor in his artistic growth as the sculptor of the fragile and impermanent.

Such catalytic experiences are what Peter L. Berger termed "signals of transcendence." As Berger explained in *A Rumor of Angels,* a signal of transcendence is an experience in our everyday world that appears to point to a higher reality beyond. Such an experience bleeps like a signal, impelling us to transcend our present awareness. The signal's message is a double one: The experience is both a contradiction and a desire. It punctures the adequacy of what we once believed while also rousing in us a longing for something surer and richer.

What is it that gives urgency to experiencing a "hole torn in life" or a "signal of transcendence"? The answer lies in our thirst for order.

For each of us, our philosophies of life express a claim about the order of the universe. The claim is crucial, for no one can live in total disorder or entirely at the mercy of arbitrary, random chance. That way lies chaos for society and madness for the individual. Any order, even tyranny, is preferable to chaos. Between our entry into life through our birth and our exit through death, each of us already feels the brevity of rushing time and the ceaseless pressure of life's limits. Any rupturing of the order is therefore life threatening. We must either repair the hole or discover a new source of order to replace the damaged one.

"I AM"

It would be a mistake to think that only negative experiences— supremely death—tear holes in life or send signals of transcendence. For Chesterton, as we've seen, it was the positive experience of gratitude for life—as far from the fear of death as one can get—that tore the hole in his earlier philosophy of seamless pessimism.

For Dostoevsky, too, the experience was extraordinarily positive— a last-minute reprieve at his scheduled execution in St. Petersburg's

Semenovsky Square in 1849. "I cannot recall I was ever as happy as on that day," he wrote later. "I walked up and down my cell in the Alekseevsky Ravelin and sang the whole time, sang at the top of my voice, so happy was I at being given back my life."

On the day of his reprieve, Dostoevsky wrote to his brother Mikhail, "When I look back at my past and think how much time I wasted on nothing, how much time has been lost in futilities, errors, laziness, incapacity to live; how little I appreciated it, how many times I sinned against my heart and soul—then my heart bleeds. Life is a gift. Life is happiness, every minute can be an eternity of happiness! *Si la jeunesse savait!* [If youth only knew]."

Like a blinding flash, Dostoevsky's reprieve lit up the truth that life itself was the greatest of all blessings. Later he would have to search for a deeper reason for his hope, but from that moment on, the contradiction of his old pessimism was undeniable and the intuition of his new hope was irresistible. He could face even the prospect of prison in Siberia with joy. His gratitude to be alive hadn't made him a believer, but he was now a searcher with a signal of transcendence to follow.

Years later the theme of gratitude for existence reemerges in Dostoevsky's last and greatest novel, *The Brothers Karamazov*. Wrongly accused of his father's murder and facing the grim prospect of prison, Mitya Karamazov talks just before his trial with his brother Alyosha: "It seems there's so much strength in me now that I can overcome everything, all sufferings, only in order to say and tell myself every moment: I am! In a thousand torments—I am; writhing under torture—but I am. Locked up in a tower, but I still exist. I see the sun, and if I don't see the sun, still I know it is. And the whole of life is there—in knowing that the sun is."

AN ATHEIST'S WORST MOMENT

Dostoevsky's elation at his reprieve is perhaps something few of us can experience to the same degree. Chesterton's gratitude, however, is more modest and closer to us. His transforming experience wasn't a reprieve before a firing squad, seeing the dawn over the Matterhorn or moonlight on the Taj Mahal, or even a connoisseur's tasting of fine music, art, or wine. Chesterton was stopped in his philosophical tracks by a dandelion and by the "thin thread of thanks" that made him grateful to be alive.

Have you ever felt that gratitude for existence? A wonder to be alive when wiggling your toes in the sand, hearing the breeze in the trees, or seeing a dewdrop on a rose? Has it ever struck you that no natural things create or sustain themselves? All of them, including you and me and the entire universe, owe their existence to something else. But to what or whom?

Experiencing at least occasionally a sheer gratitude to be alive seems to be almost universal. Of course, the feeling can be suppressed. One beautiful, sky-blue summer day, twentieth-century dramatist Samuel Beckett was drinking beer and watching a cricket match with friends. As they sat there, someone remarked that it was "the sort of day that makes one glad to be alive." Beckett immediately replied, "Oh, I don't think I would go quite so far as to say that."

Moreover, as a signal of transcendence, gratitude for being alive is not a proof but a pointer. It's an intuition, not a settled conviction. It creates a searcher, not a believer. But as Dante Gabriel Rossetti said, "The worst moment for an atheist is when he is genuinely thankful, but has nobody to thank." Or as Chesterton expressed it, "If my children wake up on Christmas morning and have someone to thank for putting candy in their stocking, have I no one to thank for putting two feet in mine?" Or again, "We thank people for birthday presents of cigars and slippers. Can I thank no one for the birthday present of birth?" As Anne Lamott says, one of the best prayers she knows is "Thank you, thank you, thank you."

It's possible that a signal of transcendence may lead nowhere. There may in the end be too great a gap between the heart that desires and the reality that disappoints. But final conclusions of any kind, positive or negative, are premature at this stage. "Holes torn in life" or "signals of transcendence," though too much for old complacencies, may not be enough for new conclusions. Yet they're vital for triggering the time for questions that begins the search for meaning.

———

Do you have the courage of your desires, or have you always considered your yearnings as idle and unproductive? Do you feel the wonder of existence, your own and that of everything? Does it truly do justice to that wonder to see it as an illusion or as a product of chance?

Let your mind and heart run deep. Come farther down the seeker's path on the long journey home.

CHAPTER SIX

CRIES TO HEAVEN, CRIES FOR HELL

"Biographies of writers," W. H. Auden once declared, "are always superfluous and usually in bad taste. A writer is a maker, not a man of action.... His private life is, or should be, of no concern to anybody except himself, his family, and his friends." Auden, the most influential English-speaking poet of his age, therefore dismissed literary biographers as "gossip writers and voyeurs, calling themselves scholars." He even proposed that writers should publish their work anonymously, so readers could concentrate on the writing rather than the writer. After he died in 1973, his executors found in his will the request that his friends burn his letters "to make a biography impossible."

But, to paraphrase Shakespeare, the gentleman doth protest too much. Even if philosophy (or poetry) is not reducible to biography, the link between life and work is too close to sever, and no one is a clearer example than W. H. Auden. Take, for instance, the illuminating incident that turned the poet into an active seeker.

UTTERLY WRONG FOR SOME REASON

Auden had come to America as a refugee from all that menaced
Europe in the 1930s, typified the very day he arrived by the news that
Barcelona had just fallen to Franco's fascist forces.

On September 1, 1939, Hitler invaded Poland, and Auden, in
New York City, wrote a poem named after the date. It began:

> I sit in one of the dives
> On Fifty Second Street
> Uncertain and afraid
> As the clever hopes expire
> Of a low dishonest decade:
> Waves of anger and fear
> Circulate over the bright
> And darkened lands of the earth,
> Obsessing our private lives;
> The unmentionable odour of death
> Offends the September night.

Auden was not a religious believer and hadn't been since he left
school, where the religion he'd encountered was "nothing but vague
uplift, as flat as an old bottle of soda water." The conviction grew in
him that "people only love God when no one else will love them." But
as World War II broke out, he knew he had to "show an affirming
flame" and make some stand for freedom. As he expressed it in the
closing lines of his poem "September 1, 1939,"

> All I have is a voice,
> To undo the folded lie.

The "hole" torn in Auden's life happened two months later. He was in a cinema in Yorkville, a largely German-speaking area of Manhattan. There he saw *Sieg im Poland,* a documentary of the Nazi conquest of Poland. When Poles appeared on the screen, members of the audience cried out, "Kill them! Kill them!" Auden was horrified.

At the time he had developed a broad blend of liberal-socialist-democratic opinions following an earlier intellectual odyssey through the dogmas of Freud and Marx. One thread had always linked his successive convictions—a belief in the natural goodness of humankind. Whether the solutions to the world's problems lay in politics, education, or psychology, once these problems were addressed, humanity would be happy because humanity was good.

Suddenly, however, watching the SS savagery and hearing the audience's brutal response, Auden knew differently. With everything in him he knew intuitively, beyond any question, that he was encountering evil and that it must be condemned. "There had to be some reason" why Hitler was "utterly wrong."

Profoundly shaken, Auden reflected on this experience over the next few weeks. His facile confidence in humanity had collapsed, just as Dostoevsky's belief in the goodness of the Russian peasant had been shattered by the peasant depravity he encountered in Siberia.

For Auden the experience opened up two troubling issues—how to account for the undeniable evil he'd encountered and how to justify its absolute condemnation. After all, there were no "absolutes" in his universe. To judge anything absolutely was naive and impossible. Philosophers had undermined absolute judgments through relativism. Psychologists had thrown it over in favor of nonjudgmental acceptance.

Auden shared his concerns with his friends. "The English intellectuals who now cry to Heaven against the evil incarnated in Hitler have no Heaven to cry to," he told one. Clearly, liberalism had a fatal flaw. "The whole trend of liberal thought," he wrote the next year, "has been to undermine faith in the absolute.... It has tried to make reason the judge.... But since life is a changing process...the attempt to find a humanistic basis of keeping a promise, works logically with the conclusion, 'I can break it whenever I feel convenient.'"

The only remedy, Auden concluded, was the necessity of a renewal of "faith in the absolute." He posed the challenge in another poem written soon after his visit to the Yorkville cinema:

> Either we serve the Unconditional
> Or some Hitlerian monster will supply
> An iron convention to do evil by.

THE CALL FOR ABSOLUTE JUDGMENT

W. H. Auden came out of the Yorkville cinema a seeker. His intuitive condemnation of the Nazi horror acted upon him just as the gratitude to be alive had moved Chesterton. It was a signal of transcendence, again with a double thrust: Auden's earlier beliefs in the goodness of humankind were exposed as woefully wrong, while a powerful desire whispered within him for justification of the condemnation of Nazism. He knew there must be an unconditional ground in the universe on which he could stand to make such a judgment. When he left the cinema, his quest was underway.

Auden's experience, in many ways so unlike Chesterton's, is just as common and just as illuminating. Ours is a world in which "Thou shalt not judge" has been elevated to the status of a new eleventh commandment. Many people today consider judging evil to be worse than doing evil. But whatever the antipathy toward "judgmentalism," there are times when the widely acclaimed attitudes of relativism, tolerance, and nonjudgmental acceptance just won't do.

Face to face with raw and naked evil, our relativism, nonjudgmentalism, and even atheism count for nothing. Absolute evil calls for absolute judgment. Instinctively and intuitively, we cry out for the unconditional to condemn evil unconditionally. The atheist who lets fly "Goddamnit!" in the face of clear evil is right, not wrong. The words are a signal of transcendence, a pointer toward a deeply desired possibility—or, if you like, a seeker's prayer.

Peter Berger calls this signal "the argument from damnation." It's the experience in which "our sense of what is humanly permissible is so fundamentally outraged that the only adequate response to the offense as well as to the offender seems to be a curse of supernatural dimensions." Instinctively we realize that failure to judge certain evils as evil is not just a theoretical failure in understanding justice but a fatal deficiency in our humanity. It's an outrage that cries out for further response: "Not only are we constrained to condemn, and to condemn absolutely, but, if we should be in a position to do so, we would feel constrained to take action on the basis of this certainty."

This was precisely what moved Dietrich Bonhoeffer to join a plot to kill Hitler—despite the theoretical toils of certain ethical misgivings: "If I see that a madman is driving a car into a group of innocent bystanders, then I can't as a Christian simply wait and comfort the wounded and bury the dead. I must try to wrest the steering wheel out of the hands of the madman."

Berger points out that because we view such condemnation as "absolute and certain," we give our judgment the status of a necessary and universal truth, and "we must look beyond the realm of our natural experience for a validation of our certainty." Looking thus "beyond," we make another discovery, as Berger observes: "Deeds that cry out to heaven also cry out for hell."

In the debate over the execution of Adolf Eichmann, architect of Hitler's Jewish extermination program, Berger notes how there was a general feeling that "hanging is not enough." But what would have been enough?

In the case of some human deeds, no human punishment is "enough"—"the doer not only puts himself outside the community of men; he also separates himself in a final way from a moral order that transcends the human community, and thus invokes a retribution that is more than human." In short, there are deeds that demand not only condemnation but damnation. The evidence that God existed, Winston Churchill once said, "was the existence of Lenin and Trotsky, for whom a hell was needed."

Today's fashionable dismissal of judgments masks a viper's nest of contradictions. We all make moral judgments all the time, knowing full well that every judgment judges also the one who pronounces it. Yet we don't like it when the same moral judgments are leveled at us. What, then, does it say of us that we persist in making moral judgments? We know, in fact, that not to make moral judgments would be impossible as well as unjust. What does it mean that, whether or not we see hell and damnation as a part of God's justice, they are unquestionably, as Berger concludes, a vindication of our own justice?

SURPRISED BY JOY

Berger's discussion of other signals of transcendence—hope, play, humor, order—is rich and varied. Others have added further examples, such as love. But no discussion of such signals would be complete without mention of the one highlighted in the story of the scholar and writer C. S. Lewis.

"All joy wills eternity—wills deep, deep eternity!" Nietzsche's Zarathustra exclaimed in his midnight song. It was precisely such an experience of joy, recurring over many years, that forced C. S. Lewis to become a seeker and a "lapsed atheist" and thrust him out on the quest for meaning that lay behind his best-selling books.

In his autobiography, *Surprised by Joy*, Lewis wrote that in a sense "the central story of my life is about nothing else." At its heart, his life was about "an unsatisfied desire which is itself more desirable than any other satisfaction." Joy, as he used the word, is sharply distinguished from both happiness, which is dependent on circumstances, and pleasure, which is always related to the senses. Joy transcends circumstances and senses. As Nietzsche said, it wills eternity. Or as Lewis described it, "I doubt whether anyone who has ever tasted it would ever, if both were in his power, exchange it for all the pleasures in the world."

One moment when Lewis tasted it occurred on a summer day when he stood beside a flowering currant bush. Suddenly and without warning the memory rose in him of a time in his old family home in Belfast when his older brother, Warnie, brought his toy garden into the nursery. He was overwhelmed by a sensation of blissful joy. "It was a sensation, of course, of desire; but desire for what? Not, certainly, for a biscuit tin filled with moss, nor even (though that came into it) for my own past—and before I knew what I desired, the desire itself was gone, the whole glimpse withdrawn, the world turned commonplace again, or only stirred by a longing for the longing that had just ceased. It had taken only a moment of time; and in a certain sense everything else that had ever happened to me was insignificant in comparison."

Desire, longing, memory, sensation—Lewis's descriptions of being surprised by joy are hauntingly evocative. But the promptings are not nostalgic, a yearning for the past. Nor can they stop and rest on any earthly object. They reach forward and higher and always out of reach—"they are only the scent of a flower we have not found, the echo of a tune we have not heard, news from a country we have never yet visited."

At first the longing for joy is a rapier-piercing desire for an "unnameable something" triggered by sensations such as the sound of a bell, the smell of a fire, or the sound of birds. But slowly we realize the grail lies beyond all human objects. No mountain we can climb, no flower we can find, no horizon we can set out for will ever fulfill our search for joy. If someone follows this quest, says Lewis, "he must come out at last into the clear knowledge that the human soul was made to enjoy some object that is never fully given—nay, cannot even be imagined as given—in our present mode of subjective and spatio-temporal existence."

THE WILL TO JOY

Is all this only sheer romanticism, on the order of the poet's "heard melodies are sweet, but these unheard are sweeter"? Is it merely wishful thinking, in the manner of Ralph Waldo Emerson's assertion that "the blazing evidence of immortality is our dissatisfaction with any other solution"? Or was the great Swiss theologian Karl Barth correct—"In every real man the will for life is also the will for joy"? Barth continues: "It is hypocrisy to hide this from oneself.... A person who tries to disbar himself from joy is certainly not an obedient person."

Such questions are legitimate, but in this first stage of the journey all fixed conclusions are premature. As with all signals of transcendence, joy raises questions; it supplies no answers. It creates seekers, not believers. C. S. Lewis, well trained in Oxford philosophy, knew too much to leap ahead of the logic of his experience. It was quite possible, he said, that reality would never satisfy this unsatisfied desire that was more desirable than any satisfaction.

At the same time, Lewis pointed out, unless these intimations are capable of fulfillment, the capacity for them is odd. Physical hunger doesn't prove someone will get bread—"he may die of starvation on a raft in the Atlantic. But surely a man's hunger does prove that he comes of a race which repairs its body by eating and inhabits a world where eatable substances exist.... A man may love a woman and not win her; but it would be very odd if the phenomenon called 'falling in love' occurred in a sexless world."

C. S. Lewis became a seeker because of joy just as Chesterton did because of gratitude and Auden because of the impossibility of not condemning evil. In the lives of each of them there was still much of the quest to cover. But the thrust of the questions tore them out of complacency, propelled them across the divide between the indifferent and the concerned, and turned them into seekers.

Reaching this point, to paraphrase Churchill, is not the end of the journey, or even the beginning of the end, but it's at least the end of the beginning. If you've responded with questions to the hole torn in your life, to the signals of transcendence you've heard, you can be sure you are among those who have begun the seeker's quest.

―――――――

Have you pondered the logic of your judgments of others, especially those times when it was utterly impossible not to judge?

Have you followed the song of your heart's desire? Wondered what would have to be if your longings are to be satisfied, not dashed, in the end?

Let your mind and heart run deep. Come farther down the seeker's path on the long journey home.

| PART TWO |

A TIME FOR ANSWERS

CHAPTER SEVEN

IS THERE A WHY?

Prisoner 174517 was thirsty. Seeing a fat icicle hanging just outside his hut in the Auschwitz extermination camp, he reached out of the window and broke it off to quench his thirst. But before he could get the icicle to his mouth, a guard snatched it out of his hands and dashed it to pieces on the filthy ground.

"Warum?" the prisoner burst out instinctively—"Why?"

"Hier ist kein warum," the guard answered with brutal finality. "Here there is no why."

For Primo Levi, Italian Jewish scientist and writer, the guard's answer was the essence of the death camps—places that defied all explanation for their absolute evil. In the face of their horror, explanations born of psychology, sociology, and economics were pathetic in their inadequacy. One could only shoulder the weight of such an experience and bear witness to the world. "Never again" was too confident an assertion. "You never know" had to be the needed refrain.

Levi later gave the impression that he had survived the poison of Auschwitz and come to terms with his nightmarish experience. One of only three returning survivors in a group of six hundred and fifty Italian Jews transported to Poland in 1944, he eventually married, had children, wrote books, and won literary prizes. His core mission, however, was always to serve as a witness to the truth, a guardian of the memory. "It is very likely," he said, "that without Auschwitz I would never have written, and would have given only little weight to my Jewish identity." But after Auschwitz, "My only thought was to survive and tell."

His most telling testimony can be read at Auschwitz itself, where the following words—requested from Levi by the Polish government for the 1980 restructuring of the Auschwitz memorial—are inscribed:

> Visitor, observe the remains of this camp and consider:
> Whatever country you come from, you are not a stranger.
> Act so that your journey is not useless, and our deaths not
> useless. For you and your sons, the ashes of Auschwitz
> hold a message. Act so that the fruit of hatred, whose
> traces you have seen here, bears no more seed, either
> tomorrow or forever after.

While some survivors of the Nazi hell later committed suicide—including Walter Benjamin, Stefan Zweig, and Bruno Bettelheim—Levi many times argued against such an act. "Auschwitz left its mark on me," he said, "but it did not remove my desire to live. On the contrary, that experience increased my desire, it gave my life a purpose, to bear witness, so that such a thing should never occur again."

Thus many people were shocked and saddened when on April 11, 1987, more than forty years after his release from Auschwitz, Primo Levi plunged to his death down the stairwell of his home in Torino, Italy.

What was it that undid Levi's mission to witness? In the opening chapter of this book I spoke of three essentials for a fulfilling life: a clear sense of personal identity, a strong sense of purpose and mission, and a deep sense of faith and meaning. To all appearances, Primo Levi possessed a clear identity and a passionate purpose. But he seemed to lack an adequate sense of faith and meaning with which to interpret and handle his harrowing wartime experience. He was an atheist when he went to Auschwitz, and the extermination camp would ever remain for him the black hole of godlessness, the extreme situation of absolute evil to which no response could ever be adequate.

For a time in 1944 he was struck by lines from Dante's *Inferno:* "Consider what you came from.... You were not born to live like mindless brutes." These words hit him "like the blast of a trumpet, like the voice of God." Two years later, restored to freedom and having met his wife, he felt he'd found at last a place in the universe where it no longer appeared "that the world was God's error."

But the dark combination of Auschwitz and atheism kept closing in on him. Levi described how he raged in silence upon hearing an old Jew thank God for having escaped deportation to the gas chambers. "If I was God," Levi said, "I would spit at Kuhn's prayer."

"If there is an Auschwitz," he wrote in his first book, *If This Is a Man,* "then there cannot be a God." Forty years later—only months before his suicide—Levi penciled a message next to that line in his copy of the book: "I find no solution to the riddle. I seek, but I do not find it."

THE FOCUSED PURSUIT

The second stage in the quest for meaning begins when we actively seek answers to the specific questions raised in the crisis of the first stage. Instinctively we know the truth of Nietzsche's words: "He who has a *why* to live for can bear with almost any *how*." Sadly for Primo Levi, he had no answer strong enough to carry the weight of his existence, no effective counter to the haunting words, "Here there is no why."

The point of the second stage is easy to see, if hard to follow. If searchers are driven by questions and some sense of need, their automatic response—consciously or unconsciously—is to pursue answers. The truth-claims of various beliefs will prove attractive or unattractive according to their power to throw light on the issues in the seeker's heart and mind.

A few aspects of this second stage deserve underscoring. First, the search for answers is essentially conceptual. Hopes, fears, hurts, and other emotions play their part, but the second stage primarily involves ideas and beliefs and the difference they make. (A seeker might even enter this stage with the express purpose of shielding emotions that have been wounded or battered during the first stage.) At this point, thinking is properly central.

This focus on ideas is in contrast not only to emotions but also to our craving for "practical action." Although ours is a pragmatic age, impatient with discussing mere ideas, we need only remember that ideas have consequences, beliefs influence behavior, differences make a difference. Seekers whose whole lives are invested in the outcome of the search know well that choices based on these ideas will not be useless or insignificant. The concepts we explore and articulate are like maps—they're only representations, but they point to solid realities just as maps lead to very real places and destinations.

G. K. Chesterton pointed to the value of such "unpractical" thought in *What's Wrong with the World:* "There has arisen in our time a most singular fancy: The fancy that when things go very wrong we need a practical man. It would be far truer to say that when things go very wrong we need an unpractical man. A practical man means a man accustomed to merely daily practice, to the way things commonly work. When things will not work, you must have the thinker, the man who has some doctrine about why they work at all."

Furthermore, the search—although obviously quite open about possible answers—is nevertheless clearly focused. There's no uncertainty about the seeker's specific questions, and any answer worthy of attention must show definite promise of satisfying them. That's the unchanging condition for an answer's worthiness; it's always a case of "Will this prove to be what I'm looking for?"

Finally, the search for answers is comparative. Occasionally a seeker will be satisfied with the first answer encountered. More often, with so many guides and maps on offer, searchers must shop around before settling on the answer that attracts them and meets all their requirements. For the seeker, contrast is the mother of clarity.

FAMILIES OF FAITH

These points are straightforward, but they're often shouldered aside by the force of either of two contradictory objections: Some people say the weighing of answers is unnecessary because all beliefs, at their core, are the same; others say the search for answers is impossible simply because there are too many beliefs to investigate, let alone appraise with care. The truth lies between these extremes.

Answering the first objection, no one has yet given a satisfactory definition for any "common core" in all beliefs. Even the word *God* (or *god*) means quite different things to an Orthodox rabbi, an African witch doctor, and a Hindu guru. These differences are more than theoretical and make an enormous difference in practice.

As for the second objection, the fact is that while there are countless beliefs in the world, there are only a few "families of faith," a term referring to all beliefs sharing the same view of ultimate reality. Different belief systems within each family have important resemblances that loom above the obvious range of genuine diversity.

For all practical purposes, there are three leading families of faith in the modern world. The Eastern family of faiths includes Hinduism, Buddhism, and New Age thought. Their common view of ultimate reality could be termed the "undifferentiated impersonal," or an impersonal ground of being. The Western secular family of faiths includes atheism, naturalism, and secular humanism. Their common view of ultimate reality is "chance plus matter plus time." Third is the biblical family of faiths, including Judaism, the Christian faith, and Islam, whose shared view of ultimate reality is an "infinite, personal God."

I'm not saying that differences *within* families of faith are unimportant—for example, between Bhakti Hinduism and Zen Buddhism, or between Orthodox Judaism and Liberal Protestantism. But what reduces the search to a manageable size are the differences found on a higher level, differences that sharply distinguish the three major families. It is these the seeker confronts and assesses first.

EVIL, FOR EXAMPLE

To each of these main families of faith we can pose the questions of life. Thoughtful seekers have raised issues about the origin and design of the universe, the existence and character of God (if there is one), the nature and dignity of our humanness, the dilemma of evil, the possibility of salvation (or liberation), what constitutes an ethical life, our prospects after death, the destiny of our planet, and so on. But no seeker wants or needs to explore all these issues. As we've seen, each seeker is driven by his or her own quest, central to which is the answer to one burning question tossed up by life.

Let us then, for the sake of illustration, take one issue—the dilemma of evil, suffering, and death—and explore in outline how the three main families of faith differ in viewing it.

Why that issue? For one thing, we're within living memory of the most evil and murderous years in history, years that saw two savage world wars, monstrous totalitarianism of the right and the left, and the genocides of Auschwitz and Cambodia.

For another, there's a huge gulf in modern society between the visibility of evil and the deficiency of intellectual and moral tools to deal with it.

For yet another, this topic raises the deepest and most agonizing questions for many of us. Our answers here are the very closest we come as human beings to unriddling life.

Finally, each of the great philosophies of life is at its crux an answer to evil and suffering. In fact, the differences in how the three families of faiths address this topic are striking. Clearly these differences make a great difference—not only for individuals but for whole societies.

Two things must always be borne in mind when exploring different answers at this stage of the search. First, each faith or philosophy deserves to speak for itself rather than being understood only through the words of outsiders or critics. As Herman Wouk reminds us, "If a way of life be judged by its misinterpreters, which way will stand?" My discussion here should therefore be seen as illustrative only.

Second, each faith and philosophy should be understood in its best form rather than its worst. As Albert Camus put it, "One should not judge a doctrine through its by-products but through its peaks." Needless to say, it is important for a searcher to examine the link between beliefs and behavior. But if we see what we consider to be bad behavior by practitioners of a belief, we do well to remember that while some behavior is an accurate reflection of that belief, other behavior is such a contradiction of it that it is no reflection at all.

A TEST OF OUR MATURITY

Let's return to the guard's brutal assertion to Primo Levi—"Here there is no why." Was there, in fact, a "why" to the death camps? Is there a "why" to evil and suffering?

Prior to the twentieth century, the defining event considered the worst betrayal of human nature and ideals was the Reign of Terror in the French Revolution. But two centuries later the Reign of Terror was dwarfed in significance by the *Shoah,* or Holocaust. The Nazi death camps became the midnight hour of human evil in history.

And it was again in Auschwitz, the nadir of human depravity, that a survivor proposed a "maturity test" for facing up to human evil. January 1995 was the fiftieth anniversary of the Allied liberation of Auschwitz, and one of the most moving public meditations was by Arnost Lustig, writer and professor of literature.

For survivors like himself, Lustig said, there was a difference between memories of Auschwitz during the day and memories that came by night. For visitors to the site, there was an even more horrific gap—between those who see it now as a museum and those who knew it as a death factory. Lustig therefore wished that somehow all men and women on earth could be sent to visit Auschwitz "for a day, an hour, or even a single second" during the time when the death camp was actually operating. Such a visit, Lustig explained, would provide "a test of maturity before they received a driver's license or be allowed to vote or get married.... I believe that this peek into hell would ripen their image of the world, for only those who have seen how little is needed to peel what is human from us—to turn us again into animals—can understand the world into which we are born."

Would that be a fair test? Having heard Lustig's proposal discussed in a variety of settings, I believe most people would find it eminently fair, not only for gauging someone's maturity, but also for proving the validity of that person's faith (or philosophy or world-view). It would offer a challenge to realism as well as to hope: First, does this faith have a realistic view of evil that allows its believers to look evil in the eye and pronounce it as evil? Second, does this faith also allow its believers to respond actively to evil with some genuine hope of countering it, perhaps even overcoming it in some way?

"Life is hard to bear," Freud wrote in *Civilization and Its Discontents*. We're threatened with suffering from three directions: from our own bodies, doomed to decay and death; from the external world, which unleashes against us the overwhelming forces of nature; and from other human beings. Auschwitz, then, is only the razor-sharp edge of a wider constellation of questions that confronts us as human beings. The issue, Dallas Willard points out, is not just "when bad things happen to good people." It should also include when bad things *don't* happen to good people, when bad things don't happen to bad people, and when good things happen to bad people.

As we look at how the three different families of faiths respond to the dilemma of evil, our discussion will be necessarily selective. We'll look only at the central features. But just as a sip of wine can be suggestive of the grapes, the vineyard, and the soil behind it, so even a sampling of ideas can point to issues far beyond the topics discussed.

Will our discussion be offensive to some? Unavoidably. It isn't fashionable to affirm that differences make a difference, that ideas have consequences, that contrast is the mother of clarity—but such perspectives are vital both to the welfare and durability of our civilization and to every seeker's personal integrity in this second stage of the quest for meaning.

———

Do you have a sufficient "why" to help you bear your "hows"?

Do you believe there's a common core to all beliefs if you dig deep enough? Or have you followed the contrast between your views and others until you see the practical consequences?

Could you look at evil with unblinking realism? Have you thought through your grounds for combating it?

Let your heart and mind run deep. Consider well the crossroads on the long journey home.

CHAPTER EIGHT

NIRVANA IS NOT FOR EGOS

It was one of the most poignant moments in Asian history, a turning point expressed in a look.

He had made up his mind after a long period of thought and indecision. But there was still the cost to consider. As far as riches, honor, and his position were concerned, the price was cheap; these things were baubles to him. His wife and son were another matter. They were his passion and delight, and the choice here cut deep. So deep, in fact, that even after making the decision, he had promised himself one last moment alone with them, but only if they were asleep and he was unseen.

So it was that he slipped into the bedroom where his wife lay sleeping with the child of their love in her arms. Desire swelled in his heart. He longed to take the infant into his arms once more and leave a parting kiss that would print a father's love on him forever. He longed to take his wife in his arms and love her with a wild, sweet passion that would nourish them both in the long, lonely miles ahead.

But it couldn't be. He stood in the shadows gazing at them, and his heart grieved. The pain of parting overcame him powerfully. Although his mind was determined—nothing, either good or evil, could shake his resolution—the tears flowed freely from his eyes.

Finally he suppressed his feelings, tore himself from the scene, and walked swiftly to where his horse and servant stood waiting at the gate.

"Do not leave now, my lord," a woman's voice cried out in the darkness. "In seven days time you will be ruler over four continents and two thousand islands. This is no time to leave."

"Well do I know it," he replied without stopping. "But it is not sovereignty I desire. I will become a Buddha and make all the world shout for joy."

THE ONLY DEAD MAN?

Thus the young Indian prince Siddhartha Gautama, known later to the world as the Buddha, or the Enlightened One, rode out into the night and into history. He "renounced power and worldly pleasures," according to one account, "gave up his kingdom, severed all ties, and went into homelessness. He rode out into the silent night, accompanied only by his faithful charioteer Channa. Darkness lay upon the earth, but the stars shone brightly in the heavens."

Brought up the son of a rajah of the Sakya tribe in Nepal, Siddhartha had led a life that was not only privileged but pampered. His father surrounded him with every conceivable pleasure and shielded him from all sorrow and suffering, with the intention "that no troubles should come nigh him; he should not know that there was evil in the world."

Three things, however, tore holes in the naiveté woven so assiduously by his father and made Siddhartha a seeker with questions about suffering. The first and deepest experience grew from the knowledge of his mother's death upon giving him birth. She had died that he might live—this left a heartache he could not escape.

The second experience occurred when he was nine. Siddhartha was taken out to watch the annual Sakya plowing festival, where his father made the first ceremonial cut into the ground. Instead of admiring his father's regal splendor, the sensitive young prince saw only the ground gashed open, insects hurtled from their habitat, worms cut in pieces, and birds descending to eat the squirming creatures on the broken soil. He was appalled and felt the suffering in his soul.

The third experience came years later when Prince Siddhartha, now grown, set out to see the world in a jewel-fronted chariot, on a route carefully decorated and arrayed by his father so as to show him only the beauties and pleasures of life. Along the way, however, he encountered first an old man, then a sick man, and finally a corpse. On seeing the corpse, Siddhartha is said to have asked, "Is this the only dead man, or does the world contain other instances?"

"All over the world, it is the same," his charioteer replied with a heavy heart. "He who begins life must end it. There is no escape from death."

"Oh, worldly men!" Siddhartha exclaimed, as if addressing his father and all others who were caught up in diversions. "How fatal is your delusion! Inevitably your body will crumble to dust, yet carelessly, unheedingly, ye live on." From then on, the son he left behind became Rahula ("the fetter"), and Siddhartha himself became "the stream enterer," whose goal was to have no self and become the Tathagata (the one who had quite simply "gone").

THE GREAT DEATHLESS LAKE

The story of Siddhartha Gautama's journey from privilege to disillusionment, to asceticism, and finally to enlightenment under the tree in Buddh Gaya, Bihar, is prototypical of the detachment toward suffering in the Eastern family of faiths. In both Hinduism and Buddhism, suffering is seen as basic to human life. Many Hindus, probably the majority, choose to pursue salvation through sacrifices, but the more thoughtful Hindu minority and the majority of Buddhists reject the sacrificial tradition and pursue the goal of Nirvana—the blowing out of the fires of all desires and the absorption of the individual self into the infinite, "the great deathless lake of Nirvana."

The clearest expression of this is Buddha's "Setting in Motion the Wheel of Dharma," in which he introduces the "Four Noble Truths." He taught this to his first five followers at the Isipatana Deer Park, near Benares, soon after his enlightenment. For twenty-five hundred years, Buddhists have revered it as the heart of his message and the defining moment in his mission.

Buddha begins by highlighting two ways of life that don't work. On the one hand, self-indulgence—whether through drugs, alcohol, overeating, or sexual promiscuity—causes more problems than it solves. On the other hand, self-mortification—through such practices as fasting, solitude, and going without sleep—is not an effective path to happiness. "Avoiding these two extremes," Buddha says, "I have realized the Middle Path."

This Middle Path is the way of Right View, Right Thought, Right Speech, Right Action, Right Livelihood, Right Effort, Right Mindfulness, and Right *Samadhi* (or concentration). And the four essentials behind these eight steps are the Four Noble Truths: *dukkha* (affliction), *samudaya* (cravings), *nirodha* (containment), and *marga* (the right track).

Clearly, attitudes toward suffering are more than just a part of Buddhism; Buddhism itself is one grand response to suffering. The first Noble Truth is the reality of affliction. "This is the Noble Truth about *dukkha*. Birth is *dukkha*. Aging is *dukkha*. Sickness is *dukkha*. Death is *dukkha*. Sorrow, pain, grief, and despair are *dukkha*. Not getting what one wants is *dukkha*. In short, the whole process of attachment is *dukkha*." In other words, bad things happen; they happen to us all in some measure; and they're part and parcel of reality as we know it.

Most people, then, would agree that Buddhism passes the "realism requirement" in Arnost Lustig's maturity test. But what of the "hope requirement"? Here opinions differ sharply, even among Buddhists. For as they themselves admit, their answer to suffering is radical, even drastic. In the words of an American Buddhist, "Buddhism is not a superficial palliative."

As the majority of Buddhists see it, the First Noble Truth establishes the human problem—affliction and suffering. The Second Noble Truth points to its cause—craving, desire, or attachment. The Third Noble Truth then highlights the way to overcome suffering through containment or extinguishing desire. And the Fourth Noble Truth describes the path to the end of desire, which in turn brings about the end of suffering. Thus "disease" is followed by "diagnosis," which is followed by "prescription," which is followed by "treatment," until suffering is overcome. Or in the words of a sacred Buddhist text,

On the cessation of sensation ceases desire;

On the cessation of desire ceases attachment;

On the cessation of attachment ceases existence;

On the cessation of existence ceases birth;

On the cessation of birth ceases old age and death,

sorrow, lamentation, grief, and despair.

Thus does this entire aggregation of misery cease.

A COLLISION COURSE

The Buddhist remedy for suffering is clearly drastic. If "the great deathless lake of Nirvana" is a state of extinguishedness, what is extinguished is not only suffering but attachment, desire, and—finally—the individual who desires. It is significant, Buddhists say, that the moment the Buddha achieved enlightenment under the bodhi tree, Gautama did not cry, "I am liberated," but, "It is liberated." He had transcended himself and become the "not-self."

There is no remedy for suffering in this world. Nor is there any prospect of a coming world without suffering. There isn't even the hope that you and I will ever live free of suffering. And finally, there isn't a you or an I. As Buddhagosa said of his state of enlightenment, "I am nowhere a somewhatness for anyone." There is only the nobility of the compassion of the enlightened on their road to the "liberation" of extinction. As G. K. Chesterton noted, "Christ said, 'Seek first the kingdom and all these things shall be added unto you.' Buddha said, 'Seek first the kingdom and then you will need none of these things.'"

The modern world raises a titanic challenge at this point for the

Eastern family of faiths. These faiths are essentially world-denying, whereas the modern world is essentially world-affirming. The inescapable contradiction need not mean the East is wrong, but it does put it on a collision course with the force and flow of the modern world. Which means, in turn, that the tendency is for modern people to respond to the Eastern faiths in one of two ways: Either they admire and maintain the tough world-denying character of the East, but use it as "refugee ideology" by which to escape the unwanted pressures of modern life, or they maintain the world-affirming character of the modern world and adapt Eastern ideas and practices to a Western framework, losing in the process the more radical traditional features of the East.

An example of the first response is the fact that many Westerners pursuing Eastern ideas and practices are clearer about what they reject in the West than about what they embrace in the East. They dislike the rush and noise of the West, for example, but keep their yoga to the level of a workout in the gym rather than a decisive step on the path to extinguishing the self.

As an example of the second response, baby boom Buddhism is increasingly touted in the West as a "religion of hope" and offered as a "spirituality for activists," whereas traditional Buddhism has no vision whatever of a world entirely just and affliction-free. Or again, the Four Noble Truths are reduced to "an authentic way of living life as it really is," or an "optimum way of mental health free of self-defeating views"— as if Buddha was an Asian Marcus Aurelius, his "right-mindedness" a handy precursor to psychotherapy and the positive thinking of Norman Vincent Peale, and Buddhism was a new market image for humanism.

Is Buddhism a satisfactory remedy for suffering, or is the cure worse than the disease? What, if any, is the place of hope? All of us will have to make up our own minds.

EXCARNATION, NOT INCARNATION

The grand challenge of a world-denying faith in a world-affirming age is starker still for Hinduism. Take the implications of its view of ultimate reality for the vital concept of individual human dignity.

If the final reality in the universe is the "undifferentiated impersonal," or ground of being (god or Brahman), what are we humans? Who are you? Who am I? Why does an individual matter? The answer of the great ninth-century Hindu philosopher Shankara is straightforward: The relationship of god to the world is that of a dreamer to his dream. The dreamer alone is real; the world is unreal. The world of our experience is therefore *maya,* a world of illusion, ignorance, and shadow—a world where individuality and diversity are thought to be real but are not. God as the ultimate reality plays hide-and-seek with himself, "freaks out" at the end of the cosmic dance, or simply forgets himself. "This is the magic power of God by which he himself is deluded," says Shankara. In other words, the world is considered real only because of our ignorance. "Brahman alone is real; the phenomenal world is unreal, or mere illusion."

Hinduism obviously has radical implications for science, but also for individuality and human dignity. Are there grounds for human rights and the inalienable dignity of each individual? Shankara's answer is simple: "Who are you? Who am I? Whence have I come? Who is my mother? Who is my father? Think of all this as having no substance; leave it all as the stuff of dreams."

What are we? We are the extension of god's essence into the world of diversity in the sense of the dream, the dance, or hide-and-seek. Humans are "God's temporary self-forgetfulness," says Radakrishnan, the former president of India. Alan Watts explains, "God entranced himself and forgot the way back, so that now he feels himself to be man, playing—guiltily—at being God." The true self is god, and the "I" that each of us considers ourself to be is really the "not-self" caught in the world of illusion, bondage, and ignorance.

It follows then that freedom is liberation from illusion—the "not-self" assimilated into the "true self" of the ground of being. As the Upanishads explain, just as pollen merges with honey, just as salt dissolves in seawater, just as the Ganges flows into the Bay of Bengal, so the divine spark in humanity is freed by its merging with the Absolute.

In short, if God alone is the "true self" and individuality is never more than the mistaken "not-self," individuality and freedom are contradictory. Freedom within Hinduism can never be freedom to be an individual. Freedom is always freedom *from* individuality. As Lord Krishna says in the Bhagavad-Gita, humanity must be cut from "the dark forest of delusion." Or as D. T. Suzuki, the Zen teacher, said, the goal of Zen is not incarnation but "excarnation."

Lewis Carroll expressed this position playfully in *Through the Looking Glass*. Speaking of the dreaming King, Tweedledee says, "And if he left off dreaming about you, where do you suppose you'd be?"

"Where I am now, of course," says Alice.

"Not you!" Tweedledee retorts contemptuously. "You'd be nowhere. Why, you're only a sort of thing in his dream."

And Tweedledum adds, "If that there King was to wake, you'd go out—bang! Just like a candle!"

OUR PROBLEM IS EXISTENCE

This view of ultimate reality means that neither traditional Hinduism nor traditional Buddhism shows the slightest concern about human rights. Entirely logical within their own frame of thinking, they regard the Western passion for human rights as a form of narcissism as well as delusion. R. C. Zaehner, who followed Radakrishnan in the Spaulding Chair of Eastern Religions and Ethics at Oxford University, underscored the point bluntly. "In practice it means that neither religion [Hinduism or Buddhism] in its classical formulation pays the slightest attention to what goes on in the world today."

Once again, my point here is not to argue that Hinduism and Buddhism need be wrong because of this view. Each seeker must decide that for himself. My concern with the contrasts is twofold.

First, the contrasts provide an opportunity to underscore again how differences make a difference. Certainly, if the Eastern family of faiths is right, both the Western secularist family and the biblical family are wrong. Human rights are an illusion. Inalienable dignity is a conceit. The Eastern family contradicts the other two families sharply. Both sides cannot be right, and the consequences of their differences are plain.

Second, the contrasts highlight the difference between examining the Eastern religions on their own terms and diluting the Eastern religions to make them palatable for Western consumption. If the superficiality of much New Age thinking is an indication, our Western tendency is to trivialize the Eastern religions and turn them into a Disney ride to the Orient.

The same taming tendency happens to sternly pessimistic thinking of all kinds. It can always be turned into a consumer fashion. Samuel Beckett's pessimism, for example, was Eastern in its content and its severity. "The major sin is the sin of being born," he asserted, echoing the Eastern view. Our real problem is existence itself. It isn't what we do but who we are.

But who in the West would swallow such pessimism, unless sweetened? So over the years Beckett's plays were slowly sentimentalized. Eventually, as one of his loyal drama critics pointed out, audiences began to delude themselves into thinking that at bottom his plays were jolly good fun. "Well, they are not jolly good fun," wrote Harold Hobson, theater critic for the London *Times*. "They are among the most frightening prophecies of, and longing for, doom ever written."

In the same way it's time to protest the Western trivializing of the Eastern religions, their tailoring for a New York magazine article or a California hot tub, as if they were simply a dash of curry to flavor the chicken soup for the Western soul. Eastern religions are one of the modern world's three great families of faith—time-honored in their age and history, rigorous in their thought and practice, and powerful in their cultural influence. The way lies open for the seeker to explore but not to cheat. Checking out answers means following their logic to the very end.

Is there a "why" here? Do you consider Hinduism and Buddhism realistic in their analysis of suffering and affliction? Are the Noble Truths an effective cure, or is the remedy worse than the disease? What difference would your answers make to the way you live?

Let your heart and mind run deep. Consider well the crossroads on the long journey home.

CHAPTER NINE

I DO IT MY WAY

The author of the essay called it his "gospel," but few readers have found any good news in it. It was written in Florence, but by a writer with an embarrassing lack of appreciation for the arts. Its setting was the gracious home of his hospitable hosts, but its tone is characterized by the bleak loneliness of the author's own heart, and he later said the essay was "only for people in great unhappiness."

In short, Bertrand Russell's "A Free Man's Worship" had unlikely beginnings. But when it was published in 1910, it was immediately hailed as a tour de force—a powerful, lyrical, impassioned statement of life without God on planet Earth. Soon it was being quoted as if the author were Pericles or Shakespeare. Eventually it was celebrated as the leading manifesto of humanism in the twentieth century.

Russell wrote the essay in 1902 in i Tatti, the beautiful villa above Florence owned by his brother-in-law, Bernard Berenson, legendary art historian and critic. Russell's loneliness was made all the bleaker by observing Berenson's devotion to his wife, Mary (the sister of Russell's wife, Alys). Berenson had married her after a passionate affair. By contrast, Russell found himself locked in a loveless marriage that was tearing him apart.

Russell described Alys as an "intellectual ball and chain" and their relationship as "long years in prison." Meanwhile he experienced what he called his "first conversion," which brought him a profound new abhorrence of violence and a sudden new love for humanity, especially children. The transformation grew not from any spiritual experience, however, but from a relationship with the wife of Alfred North White-head, his collaborator in writing *Principia Mathematica*.

In his friendship with Evelyn Whitehead, Russell became acutely aware of her "utter loneliness, filled with intense tragedy and pain." With the secret of her suffering locked inside him, Russell endured a year of emotional warfare that drove his wife close to suicide and himself toward the edge of insanity. "Strange, the isolation in which we all live," he wrote to Gilbert Murray. "What we call friendship is really the discovery of an isolation like our own, a secret worship of the same gods."

Russell's repeated use of religious language in describing his love life—conversion, gods, and so on—points to the fact that his search for love was closely linked to his loss of faith. He was appalled by the overpowering piety of his elderly grandmother, who had raised him after the death of his parents. Her faith was not only claustrophobic but anti-intellectual. She squashed all hints of her brilliant grandson's budding philosophical interests with her favorite put-down: "What is mind? No matter. What is matter? Never mind." Not surprisingly, Russell declared himself a devout agnostic two days after his sixteenth birthday. But he never lost a sense of mysticism, and in the relationship with Evelyn Whitehead he gained a new passion for love as the only force capable of filling his empty heart.

So Russell arrived in Florence to spend Christmas in 1902. His near desperation was in savage contrast to the beautiful villa with its cypress-covered hillsides echoing the deep-toned Italian bells, and to the honeymoon-like love of the Berensons. Nor did the cultural richness of Florence bring any solace. "I am a good British philistine," he confessed to Berenson, whose dazzling tour of the Uffizi left Russell unmoved. "I've looked at everything you wanted me to look at; I've listened to all you've said; but the pictures still don't give me the funny feeling in the stomach they give you."

Indeed, Russell confided in a letter, though the Berenson house was exquisitely furnished, "the business of existing beautifully, except when it is hereditary, always slightly shocks my Puritan soul."

Such was the setting for Bertrand Russell's great tract on humanism—the misery of his marriage, the trauma of his discovery of Evelyn Whitehead's lonely suffering, the ecstatic happiness of his hosts, and the idyllic beauty of his environment. "The human surroundings were ideally the worst," he remembered later, "but I spent long days alone on the hillsides & in the groves of olive and cypress, with the Arno below & the austere barren country above."

The essay, Russell admitted, was his way of working out the shock that had made him "suddenly and vividly aware of the loneliness in which most people live, and passionately desirous of finding ways of diminishing this tragic isolation." He began with Mephistopheles' account of the world to Dr. Faust. Having set down the human problem as he saw it, he gave his celebrated answer. Man, he wrote, "is the product of causes which had no prevision of the end they were achieving." Man's "origin, his growth, his hopes and fears, his loves and his beliefs, are but the outcome of accidental collocations of atoms," and therefore "no fire, no heroism, no intensity of thought and feeling, can preserve an individual life beyond the grave."

He saw that "all the labours of the ages, all the devotion, all the inspiration, all the noonday brightness of human genius are destined to extinction in the vast death of the solar system, and that the whole temple of Man's achievement must inevitably be buried beneath the debris of a universe in ruins." He concluded that "all these things, if not quite beyond dispute, are yet so nearly certain, that no philosophy which rejects them can hope to stand. Only within the scaffolding of these truths, only on the firm foundation of unyielding despair can the soul's habitation henceforth be safely built."

THUS I WILLED IT

"A Free Man's Worship," and Russell's life behind the words, take us straight to the heart of the second great family of faiths—Western secularism (or humanism or naturalism). In certain circles the word "humanism" has become pejorative rather than descriptive, but there's no doubt that a secular form of humanism is one of the most powerful faiths in the modern world.

There are different accounts of the rise of humanism—from the religious humanism of the Renaissance through the Enlightenment to today—but there's no question that secular humanism became prominent in the nineteenth century and dominant in educated circles since then.

At the same time, the central place of God in the world has been taken over by humanity. "Man is the measure of all things," Protagoras had said in the fifth century B.C. "A man can do all things if he will," Leon Battista Alberti had said during the Renaissance. In the nineteenth century this confidence matured and climaxed in a belligerent, all-out anti-God campaign, as typified by Algernon Swinburne's "Hymn of Man": "Glory to Man in the highest! For Man is the Master of Things."

Usually, however, the tone of secular humanism was more urbane and assured. Count Saint-Simon instructed his valet to wake him every morning with the words, "Arise, your highness, great deeds are to be done." "Man makes himself," said archeologist Gordon Childe. "We see the future of man as one of his own making," said geneticist H. J. Muller. "Today, in twentieth century man," Sir Julian Huxley remarked, "the evolutionary process is at last becoming conscious of itself.... Human knowledge worked over by human imagination is seen as the basis to human understanding and belief, and the ultimate guide to human progress." "All man's problems were created by man and can be solved by man," John F. Kennedy declared in his inaugural address.

Humanism's all-decisive claim is that, since there is no God, there is no revealed meaning. Therefore meaning isn't disclosed or even discovered. It's created. Human beings are both the source and standard of their own meaning, so it's up to each of us to create our own meaning. As Nietzsche asserted in *Ecce Homo,* instead of a passive life summed up in the words "it was," we must so live that we can say, "Thus I willed it." In the words of his Russian-American disciple, philosopher and novelist Ayn Rand, "My personal life is a postscript to my novels; it consists of the sentence: '*And I mean it.*'" In Russell's picture, each of us is Atlas carrying the world of our own meaning on our own shoulders. Or as Frank Sinatra put it simply, "I did it my way."

The World As We Find It

What does this view of life mean for humanist responses to suffering and evil? What are the salient features of such a response?

There is no orthodoxy in secular humanism and therefore no end to the possible variations that may claim the name. But across the prominent examples of the philosophy, two features of its response to suffering stand out.

The first feature is the frank acknowledgment that suffering and evil are part and parcel of the inhospitable universe in which humans find themselves. In Russell's vision, we're not only the product of blind chance, we're moving toward an end that contradicts and cancels out purpose—the "extinction" that he saw as the destiny of "all the labours of the ages, all the devotion, all the inspiration, all the noonday brightness of human genius."

The same point can be expressed less bleakly, but it remains the same point. I well remember as a university student meeting and listening to Bertrand Russell, then in his early nineties. Sometimes I admired the grandeur of his courage in describing such bleak realities; more often I was chilled by the arctic quality of his conclusions.

At the time, I found Albert Camus with his philosophy of the rebel far more appealing. Camus's call to fight the "plague" heroically, one patient at a time, struck chords with our passion in those days. It excited our sympathy for victims of evil. It appealed to our outrage at the state of a world gone awry.

But in the end, of course, Camus's vision was no different. When his character Dr. Rieux in *The Plague* claims that he's on the right track "in fighting against creation as he found it," he acknowledges the same reality as Russell. The flaw is in the world as we find it. Evil is natural to our world. Describe it as we wish, fight it as we can, but what we confront is still the universe as it is. All the warm-blooded outrage and compassion in the world cannot mask the nature of things. Whatever we desire, the absurd is what we discover. We simply cannot get round it. Within the humanist view, as in the Eastern view, evil is normal and natural in the world as we know it.

ENNOBLING OUR LITTLE DAY

Camus's call to rebel introduces the second prominent feature of the Western secularist response to suffering. Given the flaws and evil and suffering in "creation as we find it," it's up to us to create and shoulder our own meaning and to ennoble life by working resolutely for reform. Here the Western secularist answer decisively parts company with the Eastern answer. Suffering is part and parcel of life—on that they both agree. But far from withdrawing as the East does, the Western secularist answer is engagement, working to build, to fight, to leave the world a better place regardless of the final outcome.

Although Russell later rejected the lyrical, rhetorical style of "A Free Man's Worship," many were inspired by the essay's call to the free man to "ennoble his little day." United only by the "tie of a common doom," fully aware that life is "a long march through the night," and conscious that our comrades are vanishing one by one—"seized by the silent orders of omnipotent death"—we must still, said Russell, shed "over every daily task the light of love."

Did Russell live this altruistically himself? Not exactly. In private he later expressed reservations about the essay's ethic. "I wrote with passion & force, because I really thought I had a gospel," he said.

"Now I am cynical about the gospel because it won't stand the test of life." When Joseph Conrad wrote to congratulate him for the essay, Russell told his mistress, Ottoline Morrell, that a sense of shame came over him. "No, the man who wrote that is not the man Conrad sees now—the affection he gives is not now deserved—the man who would face a hostile universe rather than lose his vision has become a man who will creep into the first hovel to escape the terror & splendour of the night."

Commenting on the essay twenty-five years later, Russell wrote, "Fundamentally, my view of man's place in the cosmos remains unchanged," but he qualified the scope of his call to altruism—"in times of moral difficulty and emotional stress, the attitude expressed in this essay, is at any rate for temperaments like my own, the one which gives most help in avoiding moral shipwreck."

For Camus the rub lay elsewhere. Although we rebel and fight courageously, the outcome is always—as Dr. Rieux in *The Plague* acknowledges—"never ending defeat." The plague will always break out elsewhere. Evil will always stalk the earth again. After Dr. Rieux's friend Tarrou dies, the grief of the death chamber was at first a relief, but then it grew into a silence that "made Rieux cruelly aware that this defeat was final, the last disastrous battle that ends a war and makes peace itself an ill beyond all remedy."

TOO BAD TO BE TRUE?

It won't stand the test of life, says Russell. *Never ending defeat,* says Camus. Here we can see the modern world's grand challenge to the secularist family of faiths. These faiths appeal to society's intellectual elites (seen in George Steiner's description of agnosticism as "the established church of modernity. By its somewhat bleak light, the educated and the rational conduct their immanent lives"), but they hold little or no attraction for ordinary people. Bloodless as well as bleak, they are too cerebral for everyday life.

Nations whose leaders espouse secularist faiths are therefore likely to be both schizophrenic and repressive in an odd new way. With their elite classes at odds with both their nation's traditions as well as the beliefs and practices of ordinary people, societies dominated by secularist faiths will claim to be more free, but will actually be free only for people like their elites. Tone deafness has political implications as well as philosophical.

Russell prescribed his ethics "for temperaments like my own," but how many people are included in this sweep? How many of us, having been told the bleakness of the human prospects, will still adhere to the nobility of humanist ethics—especially if it appears that the author himself didn't? Why should we care for others as ourselves? Wouldn't it be just as consistent to eat, drink, and be merry, for tomorrow we die?

On Camus's tombstone are these words from *The Myth of Sisyphus:* "The struggle toward the summit itself suffices to fill a man's heart." But how many will find rebellion to be a satisfying reason for existence when we know from the beginning that we can never reach the summit? When we know, in terms of the myth of Sisyphus, that we can never roll the stone to the top of the hill, that even our best, highest, and ultimate efforts can end only in final defeat?

Despite their courage, the bleakness of Russell and Camus is all too clear. Russell's friend and fellow humanist H. J. Blackham once admitted: "The most drastic objection to humanism is that it is too bad to be true. The world is one vast tomb if human lives are ephemeral and human life itself is doomed to ultimate extinction." Jean-Paul Sartre put it equally bluntly: "Atheism is a cruel, long-term business; I believe I have gone through it to the end."

The very bleakness of the humanists' view may, however, be proof of their honesty and a badge of their unflinching realism. Do they pass the requirement for realism? Do they pass the requirement for hope?

All of us must make up our minds for ourselves. Again, the way lies open for the seeker to explore, but not to cheat. Exploring answers means following their logic to the very end.

———

Is there a "why" here? Do you consider the secularist faiths realistic in their analysis of suffering and afflic-tion? Is it enough to shed a little love en route to obliv-ion? Why should we even bother? What would your life be like if humanism were your philosophy?

Let your heart and mind run deep. Consider well the crossroads on the long journey home.

CHAPTER TEN

PEOPLE OF THE CROSSED STICKS

"Our rule of thumb in showing human suffering," a television producer once told me, "is that the death of a thousand people in the Third World is equivalent to a hundred people in the West, ten adults in our own country, and one child in our local community."

Caring, of course, has always been relative. Aristotle spoke for most human beings when he limited the reach of pity to "people like us." It's right and realistic, this view goes, to limit compassion to members of our own nation, our own tribe, our own group, our own family. In the scale of our sympathies, they simply weigh more.

Modern media have reinforced this relativity to the point of topsy-turviness. For each of us, my "neighbor" is always the person next to me who is in need when I come across him or her. But that's one thing for a medieval villager coming across his neighbor collapsed in the street, and quite another for viewers of the evening news seeing our thousandth image of an emaciated child from across the world, his bony hands reaching into our pockets in the comfort of our living room.

Television provides the images that fuel the imagination that arouses compassion. Many therefore credit television with waking them up to faraway suffering about which they would never have known or cared. At the same time, television not only extends our view but distorts it. Its very volume of images can overwhelm, leading to "compassion fatigue." Its style—the gravely serious right next to the commercial, the tragic cheek-by-jowl with the trivial—tends to fragment and shatter the link between what we know and what we do about it. Besides, with our surfeit of channels, what we've just tuned into can always be turned off when we feel like it.

Even here modern media are just exaggerating the age-old tendencies of the human heart. Long before television, Charles Dickens in *Bleak House* captured this hall-of-mirrors effect in his portrait of Mrs. Jellyby and her "telescopic philanthropy." This worthy humanitarian lady neglected all the bumps, scrapes, and wounds of the ragged children right under her nose because her farsighted eyes "could see nothing nearer than Africa."

In *The Brothers Karamazov,* Dostoevsky spoke of the difference between "love in action" and "love in dreams." Madame Khoklakhov gushes to Father Zossima about her loving intentions: "You see, I so love humanity that—would you believe it?—I often dream of forsaking all I have, leaving Lise, and becoming a sister of mercy."

Unimpressed, the elder tells her of a doctor he knew, who confessed frankly: "I love humanity,…but I wonder at myself. The more I love humanity in general, the less I love man in particular." Finally, after gently directing her to see the weakness of her utopian intentions, Zossima explains, "Love in action is a harsh and dreadful thing compared with love in dreams."

MOMENTS WORST AND BEST

No one need explain that distinction to Baroness Caroline Cox, a nurse, scientist, and former deputy speaker of Britain's House of Lords. To many of the world's helpless, she is "love in action" in human form, a Mother Teresa of the war-torn poor and a voice on behalf of the forgotten.

Asked to be the patron of a fund for Poland, Lady Cox insisted on going herself. It wasn't enough to be "a name on the writing paper." Since then, despite her busy life as a peer of the realm, "going herself" has meant spending ten days every month on trips to devastated places such as strife-torn Sudan or the embattled Karabakh region claimed by both Armenia and Azerbaijan.

She reaches out with food, clothes, and medicine to war victims—regardless of their color, creed, or race—who have been maimed and raped, their families robbed, killed, or taken into slavery. Often when she arrives, the people greet her with the words: "Thank God you've come. We thought the world had forgotten us."

A friend of mine once asked her to relate both her worst moment and her best during all her journeys of mercy. The worst? She thought for a moment, then described with brutal simplicity what it was like to enter a Dinka village after Sudanese government-backed soldiers had left, laden with human loot.

The stench of death was overpowering. More than a hundred corpses lay where they had been savagely butchered. Men, women, children, even cattle had been cut down or herded into captivity to be carried north as slaves. Straw huts were ablaze, crops razed, and devastation and death affronted the eyes everywhere. Worst of all was the knowledge that the militia with their gunships and Kalashnikov rifles would return, and the area's villages once again would be naked before the ferocity and blood lust of the fundamentalists from the north. "Genocide is an overworked word," Baroness Cox said, "and one I never use without meaning it. But I mean it."

And her best moment? This, she said, came right after the worst. With the raiders gone and the results of their cruelty all around—husbands slain, children kidnapped into slavery, homes ruined, and they themselves brutally raped—the few women still alive were pulling themselves together. Their first instinctive act was to make tiny crosses out of sticks lying on the ground and to push them into the earth.

What were they doing? Fashioning instant memorials to those they had lost? No, Lady Cox explained, the crudely formed crosses were not grave markers, but symbols. The crossed sticks, pressed into the ground at the moment when their bodies reeled and their hearts bled, were acts of faith. As followers of Jesus of Nazareth, they served a God whom they believed knew pain as they knew pain. Blinded by pain and grief themselves, horribly aware that the world would neither know nor care about their plight, they still staked their lives on the conviction that there was one who knew and cared. They were not alone.

BIFOCAL VISION

Who would not be moved by the Dinka women's instinctive resort to the deepest symbol of their faith in their deepest time of agony? This story unlocks the door to the heart of the biblical family of faiths and its response to suffering. Two salient features of that response are noteworthy.

First, within the biblical family, pain, suffering, and death are viewed as abnormal, an alien intrusion rather than something natural.

The ultimate problem lies not in who we are but in what we've done—in our disobedience rather than our existence.

The roots of this conviction lie in the twin biblical doctrines of creation and the fall. Created directly out of nothing by God, the world was and remains good. But it's also fallen. The entry of moral disobedience has left the world marred and broken.

Thus the biblical vision is characteristically bifocal. The world must always be understood simultaneously from the perspective of creation and the perspective of the fall. Sometimes we see what it might have been. Sometimes we see only what it has become by being marred. Neither one lens nor the other provides focus by itself; only the two together bring clear sight.

This bifocal vision lies behind a defining feature of the biblical faiths and their significance for civilization—what C. S. Lewis calls their "blessedly two-edged character." The Christian faith, Lewis points out, has a track record of being world-affirming and world-denying at the same time.

Because of its view of creation, the Christian faith—like humanism today and Confucianism in the past—openly affirms the world. It therefore builds hospitals, encourages the arts, pursues science, and is the most powerful animating force in history's most world-affirming civilization. At the same time, because of its view of the fall, the Christian faith openly denies the world—like Buddhism and Hinduism, although for very different reasons—and therefore teaches the importance of fasts as well as feasts, self-denial as well as celebration, and the glories of heaven as well as the grandeur of the earth. Christians may at times have gone overboard on one side or the other—some becoming too worldly and others becoming too otherworldly. But the biblical position unashamedly stresses both sides together.

This bifocal vision carries a momentous implication for the

biblical response to suffering. If suffering is a result of the fall rather than creation—a consequence of what we've done rather than of who we are relative to the world as it was created to be—then pain, suffering, and death are abnormal and alien, not normal and natural. As such, they're incriminating evidence of what almost all human beings feel in the face of evil: *The world should have been otherwise.*

In his memoir, *Errata,* George Steiner describes how he reacts to the infliction of wanton pain on children and animals. He speaks of a "despairing rage," a "hot blackness," and "impotent fury." "At the maddening center of despair," he writes, "is the insistent instinct…of a broken contract. Of an appalling and specific cataclysm. In the futile scream of the child, in the mute agony of the tortured animal, sounds the 'background noise' of a horror after creation, after being torn loose from the logic and repose of nothingness. Something—how helpless language can be—has gone hideously wrong. Reality should, could have been, otherwise." The anger and guilt, he says, "master and surpass my identity" and "carry with them the working hypothesis, the 'working metaphor,' if you will, of original sin."

The philosopher Schopenhauer was often quoted as saying, "Life ought not to be"; Samuel Beckett asserted later, "The major sin is the sin of being born." Both these pessimists, blaming suffering on human existence rather than human action, moved inevitably toward the Eastern position and its implication of radical renunciation of the world. Within the Eastern perspective, after all, the problem is not death but rebirth and the constant motion of the wheel of suffering.

As George Steiner shows, the logical thrust of the biblical faiths blasts in the opposite direction. "Life ought to be otherwise," say the Jew and the Christian. Human beings may be caught in tragic situations in life, but the problem can be traced to human beings, not life.

Or to use Camus's phrase, the problem isn't in creation but in "creation *as we find it*"—its "found" condition being a later result of the fall rather than its original state.

But is all this mere wordplay?

OUTRAGE AT DEATH

I first encountered the human implications of this belief many years ago through an older and wiser friend in Switzerland. We were together when he was told the news of a well-known Christian leader whose son was killed in a cycling accident. The leader had been devastated but became the quiet admiration of all when he summoned up his strength, suppressed his grief, and preached eloquently on hope at his son's funeral. My friend quietly commented, "I trust he feels the same thing inside."

Several weeks later my friend received a telephone call from the Christian leader. Could he come and talk to him? Several of us were there and welcomed him, and he went in to talk with my friend, but after a few minutes the rest of us left the house altogether. The chalet's walls were thin, and what we heard was not the hope of the preacher but the hurt of the father—pained and furious at God, dark and bilious in his blasphemy.

My friend's response was not to rebuke him but to point him to the story of Jesus at the tomb of his friend Lazarus. The account in the gospel of John says three times that Jesus was angry. One of the words used is the Greek term for "furious indignation"—the word used by Aeschylus to describe war horses rearing up on their hind legs, snorting through their nostrils, and charging into battle. This was the reaction of Jesus of Nazareth when face to face with a loved one's death. The world that God created good and beautiful and whole was now broken and in ruins. In moments Jesus was going to do something, but his first response was outrage—instinctive, blazing outrage. Clearly, death was even worse in his eyes than in ours.

The death of a close friend and colleague prompted Larry Ellison, chairman of the Oracle Corporation, to exclaim, "Death makes me very angry. Premature death makes me angrier still." From the Jewish and Christian perspectives, such outrage is right, not wrong. Within the bifocal vision, the anger (or shock or grief) is natural precisely because the evil is unnatural. This, as C. S. Lewis observed, brings us back to the paradox of the biblical faiths: "Of all men we hope most of death; yet nothing will reconcile us to—well, its *unnaturalness*."

NO OTHER GOD HAS WOUNDS

The second salient feature of the response by biblical faiths to suffering is that we can face and fight evil because God himself both cares and comes to the aid of those who look to him. In contrast to the Eastern religions, the biblical response is one of engagement, not detachment. And in contrast to the Western secularist beliefs, we're not on our own. Precisely because of a wisdom and strength higher than anything human, those who combat wrong can have solid grounds for trusting in the final triumph of good over evil. Even when we die, God keeps faith with us in the dust.

So for Jews and Christians to sing "We shall overcome" is not whistling in the dark but a commitment to justice based on confidence in its ultimate victory. This confidence grows directly from their vision of God. Far from being an "undifferentiated impersonal," a bare "ground of being," a "cosmic force," let alone blind chance or the laws of nature, the God who addresses his creatures in the Bible is personal as well as infinite.

In contrast to those who think religious belief is a mere human projection, the God of the biblical story is not simply personal for us but personal in himself. He's personal because of his own nature, not because we need him to be personal. He isn't made in our image; we're made in his. And there's no other ground for justifying the preciousness and inalienable dignity of each human being.

No one stands taller in Jewish history than Moses, and the theme of God's personal involvement is powerful from the beginning of his mission to liberate his people. "Let my people go!" his command rings out to Pharaoh (and down the centuries to oppressed people everywhere). And behind the command: "I have indeed seen the misery of my people in Egypt," God said to Moses. "I have heard them crying out because of their slave drivers, and I am concerned about their suffering. So I have come down to rescue them from the hand of the Egyptians."

At the end of Moses' life, with the Exodus and the crossing of the wilderness behind him, Moses' wonder is deeper than ever. "What other nation is so great," he asks rhetorically, "to have their gods near them the way the Lord our God is near us whenever we pray to him?"

Whether the Torah pictures God as redeemer—the next of kin whose business is to meet every need, bear every burden, pay every price—or as the one who promises to send his Messiah, the God of the Jews is an intervening God. His heart is to step in on behalf of his people and on behalf of the poor and helpless, especially when they cry to him from under oppression.

For Christians who believe that Jesus is that kinsman-redeemer and that Messiah, their faith centers on a scandal that no time can rub smooth and no triumphs ever soften: A tortured criminal spread-eagled and naked on the instrument of his execution—for our sake. The God whom Jesus shows on the cross is one who defeats evil by letting it do its very worst to him and then overcoming it.

It was this cross that took Dostoevsky to faith through "the hell-fire of doubt." Gazing at the suffering of Jesus as he stood in front of Hans Holbein's *Descent from the Cross,* he realized the painted scene was more than graphic realism. It was a window into the reality of the universe. If God's son suffered like this, there could be redemption in the world. As Alyosha says in *The Brothers Karamazov,* "I do not know the answer to the problem of evil, but I do know love."

It was this cross that kept alive Emily Dickinson's flickering faith despite her doubts. Jesus was the pioneer even in suffering and death: "All the other Distance / He hath traversed first— / No New Mile remaineth." Or as she expressed in another poem, the piers on which believers tread may be brittle, but God "sent His Son to test the Plank, / And he pronounced it firm."

It was this cross that Duke Ellington wanted over his bed as he lay dying. His Christmas cards, which often were sent out as late as July, were mailed early that year—in May. Their design was the same as the sign over his bed. Against a brilliant blue background, gold letters spelled GOD in a horizontal line with LOVE placed vertically, forming a cross with the common O in the middle.

And it was this cross that spelled out to author Henri Nouwen "the compassionate God." Contemplating the *Isenheim Altar* by Matthias Grünewald in Colmar for more than three hours, he wrote, "I had an inkling of the reaction of the plague-stricken and dying sufferers in the sixteenth century. On this altar they saw their God, with the same suppurating ulcers as their own." God's liberation, Nouwen concluded, is not by removing suffering from us but sharing it with us. "Jesus is God-who-suffers-with-us."

No other god has wounds.

THE MODERN WORLD'S CHALLENGE

The two leading biblical faiths, Judaism and the Christian faith, have largely given rise to the modern world. Now they're both challenged to the core by that world, a challenge that calls into question the identity and authority of both of them.

For Jews the last two centuries have brought such cataclysmic changes as emancipation, the end of the ghetto, the Enlightenment, American assimilation, the rise of Zionism, the Nazi annihilation of Eastern European Jewry, the birth of Israel, the contribution of their fellow Jews to the grand ideologies of irreligion, and the yawning schism between ultra-Orthodox and secular Jews.

For Christians the same period has brought the collapse of church-state establishments, the erosion of their centuries-long cultural dominance in the West, the rise of higher critical assaults on the Bible, the growing divergence between traditional and revisionist forms of the faith, and the astonishing fact that at the end of the twentieth century the Christian faith was the most studied and the most persecuted faith in the world.

Whether these two faiths retrieve the authority of their heritages, rediscover their identity and authority, and stand together as partners to contribute to the forward movement of the civilization to which they've given rise is one of the key questions of the new century.

No one should take away the wrong lessons from the Jewish and

Christian plight in the face of the modern world. Can others presume to step forward blithely to take over the baton? Hardly. The modern world's challenge to religion is not escaped so easily. The sorry state of these two biblical faiths under the impact of modernity is actually a compliment to them and a caution to others. Those first hit by modernity are those worst hit, but this is a backhanded acknowledgment of their leadership. Similarly, those farther behind may appear to be better off, but only so long as they stay farther behind and don't engage with the challenges of the modern world.

MY CARDS ON THE TABLE

As I made clear earlier, this brief survey of the leading families of faith and their broad response to suffering is only illustrative. I've endeavored to portray them straightforwardly and accurately, although I stress again that there's no substitute for hearing about each one from its own advocates, and I don't pretend to be completely impartial.

Which faith throws the most light on the human dilemma of suffering? That's for each of us to ask and each of us to answer. But no one with an ounce of common sense can claim that all three are saying the same thing or that we can distill a common element from the three approaches. Differences make an enormous difference.

Here let me lay my own cards face up on the table. Growing up, I lived for ten years in China, a Buddhist culture, and later, after university, studied under a Hindu guru in Rishikesh in the foothills of the Himalayas. But I draw back, today more than ever, from the fundamental detachment of the Eastern response to suffering.

Equally, over the course of my life I have read, studied, and in several cases known the leading proponents of the Western secularist faiths and have lived many years in university settings—supremely Oxford—where such faith was the majority belief. But in the end I find all the varieties of secularism fundamentally bleak and tellingly deficient when it comes to the requirements for a satisfactory human life outside the academic world.

My commitment and sympathy, in short, are with the biblical family of faiths, but only after long reflection—and not before considering the third phase of the seeker's quest for meaning. We turn now to this third stage—a time for evidences, including the thorny question of truth.

———

Do you see a "why" in the biblical family of faiths? Does reality represent for you "something that should never have been" or something that "should have been otherwise"? Are you drawn by the thought of a God who is close to you and able and willing to intervene? Or would such a God be only someone to accuse for all that has gone wrong?

Let your heart and mind run deep. Consider well the crossroads on the long journey home.

PART THREE

A TIME FOR EVIDENCE

CHAPTER ELEVEN

ROADBLOCKS AND REALITY

Today my close friend Bob is a respected political and business leader in his home state. When I first met him, he was a dropout from Harvard University ("on leave of absence" might have been the official term) with a long blond ponytail well below his shoulders. As the 1960s faded and became the victim of grand myths and gross distortions, dropouts became only flower children, forlorn and feckless refugees from the real world. But there was never anything the slightest bit forlorn about Bob.

Bob and strength were synonymous. Friendly, handsome, articulate, a natural leader, a born politician, keenly interested in all that was going on in the world—he had all these characteristics in a strong way. When I met him, he was also a strong seeker, in the forefront of any discussion, trenchant in his questioning, quick with objections, relentless in following arguments to their end, and resolute in pushing himself and others toward conclusions and action. All of which catapulted him on a quest for meaning that was as strong and restless as he was.

FOR RENT CONTROL

Born a child of privilege in America's Eastern establishment, Bob had moved surefooted through elite prep schools, then found himself at Harvard. Like many young people of the time, he'd been inspired by John F. Kennedy's 1961 inaugural address; he had asked what he could do for his country and the world. He was motivated by a passion to change society. His philosophy was a conscious and articulate belief in the "moral rightness and righteousness of liberal democratic values," as he later expressed it, coupled with a Kennedyesque conviction that the answer to society's ills was getting the right people into positions of leadership.

Then came a series of personal incidents that hammered away at his view of reality. In Bob's words, they were moments that said, "No, the world is really not that way." They were "signposts that pointed to another view of reality."

In the spring of 1969, during Bob's sophomore year at Harvard, the university was convulsed in turmoil that eventually erupted when police were sent in to roust out students occupying the administration building. In response, the student body put forth a series of six demands, half in opposition to the Vietnam War and half concerning Harvard's presence in the local Cambridge community.

Bob himself had been working in the poorer area of East Cambridge and had spoken on behalf of rent control, then a brand-new concept being trumpeted as a panacea. In the activist passion of that spring at Harvard, he gave a speech on the topic to a group of students and professors. By supporting rent control, he told them, you were on the side of peace, justice, love, and the human race; if you opposed rent control, you were basically against everything good. It was a clever speech, all black and white with no grays, and loaded with buzzwords. Fired up by Bob's passionate rhetoric, the audience moved off to protest, some of them in ugly incidents at the residence of Harvard's president.

Bob was appalled. He felt a sickening realization. He had just manipulated a group of "supposedly very bright people" into believing something simply by his use of "all those clever adjectives and clever associations." He thought of an essay he'd recently written on Nietzsche's *Beyond Good and Evil,* with that association, "a light went on and I realized that the emperor had no clothes." There seemed no foundation to the beliefs of the liberal democratic values held by his friends and peers and teachers. Bob wondered: *Perhaps nothing in itself is right or good or just. We just manipulate others to think so.*

The next day Bob made his decision to leave Harvard. His belief that some things were truly right and good and just had been shaken to its core. Now he transferred the strength of his passion to searching for a new foundation—if there was one.

ONLY BIOCHEMICAL REACTIONS?

That summer Bob attended the legendary Woodstock festival and received government funding to study the new generation's burgeoning communes and free health clinics. He was unimpressed by their utopianism. Never an advocate of "flower power," he found that for all the talk of common life and free love, what held the communities together was power. Ideals were not enough. Without strong leadership, the community movement drifted into chaos and disillusionment. There was certainly no answer there.

Bob went to Europe and traveled widely. His search deepened and became philosophical as well as political and social. Some travelers' backpacks were filled with clothes; Bob's were weighed down with books by Nietzsche, Sartre, Camus, Beckett, Alan Watts, Robert Heinlein, R. D. Laing, and C. S. Lewis. The latter was added after a Christian teacher in Switzerland challenged him to live consistently with his convictions: If Bob's emerging nihilism was right, what would that mean for him in practice? This challenge to consistency slowly cut home.

While hitchhiking from Gibraltar to Stockholm, he was given a long lift by a Cambridge don and his wife. The don was a philosopher, and Bob found himself pressing their conversation toward the logical conclusion of his own philosophical position, as if challenging the Englishman to put forward an answer that they both could believe. The more Bob pressed, the less he found. The Englishman saw no meaning in the universe and reduced everything to biochemical responses.

"So you mean," Bob said, after hours of conversation between Madrid and Bordeaux, "that after all these years of marriage there has really been nothing more to your relationship than biochemical reactions and illusions of love and caring?"

"Yes," said the don, "that's right." His wife, seated next to him in the car, burst into tears.

It was an incredible moment for Bob—part triumph, part guilt. Guilt not only because he'd driven a sword between a husband and wife, but also from knowing that he did not live consistently either. He had valued love, compassion, justice, and human dignity, but on the basis of his philosophy these things had no meaning.

Later came a conversation in Stockholm with Diane, an American girl who was a close friend. She and Bob understood each other well; both knew they had no answers, so there was no need to pretend with each other. Bob revealed to her the point he had reached in his quest: Although he didn't subscribe to the biblical world-view, or even like it, he'd found no satisfactory alternative. He was coming to the conclusion that unless the biblical world-view was true, everything was meaningless.

Until then, Bob's talk of absurdity and the horror of the abyss had been just that—talk, not experience. Suddenly everything changed. "I remember the look of horror on Diane's face, and I realized with horror myself what I had done to her. She was an incredibly loving person with a smile always on her face. It was as if I had stripped it all away, and was shaking her and saying, 'You've got to see that life is absurd; life is meaningless.' Yet I was doing it to someone I cared for deeply, and I was horrified." With an intensity that needed no words, they both knew they had gone beyond peering over the edge of the abyss; they were slipping into it.

At a similar place in the search for meaning, another friend of Bob's from Harvard had blown his brains out. But Bob felt the full force of a reality more powerful than the abyss, a reality that pointed beyond absurdity—*meaning* that could not be denied. "No matter how hard I had tried to live as though life was absurd and meaningless, what I came up against again and again was meaning.... I simply couldn't live as though life had no meaning, because it did—powerfully and beautifully."

He realized that if the biblical faith was true, then there was a foundation underneath the meaning. This thought was the last thing he expected or wanted. "Yet at the same time the overwhelming sense that everything pointed this way was my last hope. Either the biblical answer was true or there was only absurdity." His search took on new seriousness and a new direction.

CHECKING IT OUT

Bob's quest raises issues that are at the heart of the third phase in the quest for meaning—a time for evidences. This stage begins when we ask whether the answer we found so illuminating at the second stage is in fact true. The answer may have thrown light on our problem, but does it have weight? On the way to discovering what *is* true, we challenge what proves to be not true.

It's the simple process of "checking it out," although some give it fancier names. Philosophers call it "verification"; lawyers term it "due diligence."

The evidence we find and consider in this stage does not create faith; it either confirms it or disconfirms it. Are there good and solid reasons to believe what we're being asked to believe? If this question isn't answered—or, worse, isn't allowed—seekers may become believers, but they will always be vulnerable to the doubt that their faith is only a projection, a form of wish fulfillment, an illusion, a crutch. We would be believing only because we need to believe—which at best is irrational and at worst dishonest.

The wiser way is to say, as Pascal does in *Pensées:* "We must then look at this in detail. We must put the evidence on the table." Or as C. S. Lewis writes in *God in the Dock:* "Christianity claims to give an account of *facts*—to tell you what the real universe is like. Its account of the universe may be true, or it may not, and once the question is really before you, then your natural inquisitiveness must make you want to know the answer. If Christianity is untrue, then no honest man will want to believe it, however helpful it might be; if it is true, every honest man will want to believe it, even if it gives him no help at all."

Does Lewis's assertion sound eminently reasonable? It certainly did to most readers when it was written, but in some circles today it would be highly controversial. No concept in the modern world is surrounded by more distortions and controversy than "truth."

THE NEW OBSCENITY

Claims to truth have always been controversial, as seen in Francis Bacon's famous quip in the seventeenth century—"'What is truth?' said jesting Pilate and didn't stay for an answer." W. B. Yeats joked that he didn't know "a single person with a talent for conviction." But in today's atmosphere of skepticism and relativism, in an era that prizes tolerance, affirms diversity, and bends over backward not to appear judgmental, serious claims to truth sound like an obscenity. They prompt embarrassed looks, rising blood pressure, and open hostility. Clearly a claim to truth today marks one as utterly intolerant, culturally gauche, and among the unwashed ranks of fanatics and bomb-throwers.

The concept of truth, however, is far too important to be surrendered to its critics. Truth is one of our simplest and most precious gifts. Without it we could not handle reality and negotiate life. It underlies our science, our politics, our journalism, our relationships, and our knowledge of all kinds.

Far from being intolerant, repressive, or unhealthy, truth is a vital requirement for free societies that would remain free. Truth matters supremely because, in the end, there is no humanness or freedom without it. In fact, truth *is* humanness and freedom. The way to a good life and a free life lies in knowing what is true and learning to live in that truth. No concept, in its place, is more essential to the seeker.

CLEARING THE FOG

"One should never put on one's best trousers to go out to battle for freedom and truth." Henrik Ibsen's homespun advice is an excellent antidote to any seeker's starry-eyed idealism. One day, we believe, truth will prevail. But today and tomorrow, truth will have to be won in the teeth of a thousand scornful dismissals.

The best way to clear the fog is to think through today's controversies over truth. Here are five considerations:

First, we must remember that over the course of history, appreciation for truth has generally prevailed over advocacy of skepticism. Although truth and skepticism have always been in tension, today's esteem of skepticism over truth is not the normal situation. We may confidently expect appreciation for truth to prevail again.

"Truth! Truth!" exulted Augustine of Hippo. "How the very marrow of my soul yearned for it." Philosophers, said Plato, are those with "no taste for falsehood; that is, they are completely unwilling to admit what's false but hate it, while cherishing the truth." "Truth or nothing" was the motto of Max Weber. "My country is truth," wrote Emily Dickinson. Albert Camus advised, "Prefer truth to everything." Such is the prized status of truth in more normal times, times that will come again.

Second, today's suspicion and skepticism toward truth is the direct result of our overreaching attempts to attain, on our own, the knowledge of certainty. Some people (rationalists) tried it on the basis of reason alone. Others (empiricists) tried it on the basis of the senses alone. Others again (logical positivists) tried it on the basis of scientific standards alone. All three approaches raised the bar too high. Rejecting any assumptions beyond human reason, they posed the conclusion as being either absolute certainty or total skepticism. Not surprisingly, human reason by itself couldn't attain absolute certainty, and the result was total skepticism. Such sophism, by the way, is hardly new. Gorgias, a sophist skeptic and critic of Socrates, claimed centuries ago that nothing exists—but if it does, it can't be understood, and if it can be understood, it can't be expressed.

Third, today's prevailing skepticism toward truth is riddled with its own contradictions and inconsistencies. Skepticism, needless to say, isn't all bad; there are countless beliefs and opinions of which we should be skeptical—much more so, in fact, than we are. But the radical skepticism that prides itself on its consistency is in fact quite inconsistent and irresponsible.

"There is no such thing as truth," the skeptic says. "Those who claim there is are arrogant and intolerant." But is his statement itself true? If not, we needn't bother with it. If it is true, then we have one example of truth that defies the claim that there is none (and any criteria that allow one statement to be true will also allow the possibility of others). Moreover, the statement is intolerant and hypocritical. It vetoes all other claims to truth while suppressing its own characteristics as a truth claim.

Fourth, only one family of faiths—the biblical family—puts a premium on the absolute importance of truth and explains why truth is anchored and reinforced in the universe itself. For Jews and Christians, truth matters infinitely and ultimately because it's a question of the trustworthiness of God himself. He is true, he acts truly, he speaks truly. Our human "truth seeking" is therefore underwritten by the truthfulness of the creator of the universe. Truth transcends us. As we follow it, it leads us on, back, and up to one who is true. Jews and Christians know why truth matters and matters absolutely.

Since we need what is called "truth directedness" for science, politics, and everyday communication, even secularists always have to act *as if* it were so. Yet in much of nature, according to the secularist view, deception must be an advantage and truth a handicap. If Darwinism, for example, is right, truth directedness at best is a leap of faith. At worst, it's part of our human alienation in a universe in which truth seeking is ultimately futile. As the paleontologist George Gaylord Simpson put it, "The meaning of evolution is that man is the result of a purposeless and natural process that did not have us in mind."

Fifth, despite all the controversies and complications, the notion of truth remains straightforward. In our ordinary speech, telling the truth is "telling it like it is." We can say then that a statement (or an idea or a belief) is true *if what it is about is as it is presented in the statement.* Belief in something doesn't make it true; only truth makes a belief true. But without truth, a belief may be only speculation plus sincerity—or perhaps, worse, bad faith. True beliefs then are beliefs that correspond with reality. What they represent as real is in fact so. That's what we mean when we say a belief is "true."

WHEN ANSWERS FAIL

Are there good reasons—is there solid evidence—for believing that the answer that best responds to our questions also corresponds to reality and truth? When the fog surrounding truth clears away, the core issue in phase three shows up clearly again. But as Bob's story and experience demonstrate, there's a close link between confirmation and disconfirmation, between evidence and counterevidence. If we become genuine seekers and look for answers to our questions, the search for the adequate answer is sharpened when other answers fail to satisfy and are shown to be inadequate or contradictory. These moments of truth that contradict certain answers are a vital part of the quest.

The reason for this point is simple: While nothing is unarguable, some thoughts can be thought but not lived. Thus, as we saw in discussing diversion, David Hume, after hours of amusement, would return to his speculations on skepticism and find them too "cold and strained and ridiculous" to pursue further. He poked his nose over the abyss but withdrew it sharply when he saw what was involved, and he went back to playing backgammon with his friends. As fellow philosopher Kathleen Knott wrote of Hume, he saved himself "by refusing to take the implications of his philosophy to heart."

Nietzsche, by contrast, looked over the edge of the abyss and plunged in. As H. J. Blackham wrote of him; "One can look down into the bottom of an abyss, refusing the possibility to throwing oneself over the edge, but one cannot explore the possibility by a tentative jump. One can examine in thought the possibility of nihilism…but if one is determined to will and to live the possibility of nihilism, then one no longer has any independent standpoint under one's feet…. One is actually sucked down and engulfed."

The challenge put to my friend Bob was to live consistently with what he believed to be true—to take his beliefs beyond conversation topics and debating points and try to live them consistently. When he couldn't or wouldn't do that, it was time to question whether those beliefs were adequate and, if not, to look for others that were.

AND YET, AND YET

Consider two incidents that are telling in themselves and have also had a profound effect on seekers I have known.

One is a description by Robert Pirsig in *Zen and the Art of Motorcycle Maintenance*, of his narrator's break with Hinduism. The narrator, Phaedrus, was in Benares in the classroom as the professor of philosophy was expounding on the Hindu view of the illusory nature of the world "for what seemed the fiftieth time." Phaedrus raised his hand and asked coldly if the atomic bombs dropped on Hiroshima and Nagasaki were only an illusion. The professor smiled and said yes. The exchange was over.

But not for Phaedrus who, like Bob, was a passionate young American in the age of the Vietnam War. "Within the traditions of Indian philosophy that answer may have been correct," Pirsig wrote. But "for Phaedrus and anyone who reads newspapers regularly and is concerned with such things as mass destruction of human beings, that answer was hopelessly inadequate. He left the classroom, left India, and gave up."

An even more poignant example of a roadblock comes from the eighteenth-century Japanese poet Issa, perhaps the best loved of all haiku poets because of the humanness of his writing. His own life was very sad. All five of his children died before he was thirty, and then his young wife died. After one of the children's deaths, he went to a Zen master and asked how he was to face such suffering.

"Remember," the master said, "the world is dew." Just as the sun rises and the dew evaporates, so on the wheel of suffering sorrow is transient, life is transient, human beings are transient. Involvement in the passion of grief speaks of a failure to transcend the momentum of selfish egoism. *Remember, the world is dew.* There is a Hindu saying: "The wise in heart mourn not for those who live, nor for those who die."

That was the master's religious, philosophical answer. But on returning home, Issa wrote one of his most famous poems:

> This dewdrop world
> a dewdrop world it is, and still,
> although it is...

Or as it might be more simply translated,

> The world is dew,
> the world is dew—
> and yet,
> and yet...

For all the distilled beauty and pathos of the poem, the thrust is piercing. *The world is dew, the world is dew*—the first lines go one way, expressing the logic of Buddhism. *And yet, and yet*—the last lines go the opposite way, expressing the heart of a father, a husband, a human being whose agonized grief and tortured love can only cry into the unfulfilled darkness where Zen sheds no light. No wonder many

Westerners on the road to the East have turned around after reading Issa's poem.

There *is* reality. And in the search for the truth of it, there are roadblocks. There are moments of truth that contradict rather than confirm. Rerouting is common. So the time for evidence and counter-evidence is all-important. At stake is the humanness and freedom of the meaning we discover for our lives.

———

Do you consider any claim to truth to be arrogant and intolerant? Have you thought through the relationship between truth, reality, humanness, and freedom? Have you followed the logic of your beliefs consistently to see where they lead? Or are your beliefs ones that can be thought but not lived?

Let your heart and mind run deep. Look closely at the confirmations and disconfirmations on the long journey home.

CHAPTER TWELVE

BIOGRAPHY AS
PHILOSOPHY

"My time has not yet come; some are born posthumously." Friedrich Nietzsche's bold prediction about himself, written only months before he slipped the last threads of his reason, was amply fulfilled. Shuttling in the 1880s between Eze-sur-Nice in France, Torino and Portofino in Italy, and Sils Maria near St. Moritz in Switzerland, and writing through incessant pain, he issued such a cataract of revolutionary and influential writings that the twentieth century has been called an extended footnote on Nietzsche.

The same claim to a "posthumous birth" could apply equally to Vincent van Gogh. Every time the auctioneer's hammer falls and another of his paintings sells for a record price, attention is drawn back to a life that was short, lonely, wretched, unsuccessful—and to an artist who was tragically misunderstood.

And still is in some ways. For although van Gogh's paintings are among the world's most popular, much of his life remains blanketed by ignorance and distortions. After all, isn't it common knowledge that van Gogh committed suicide because he suffered from extreme schizophrenia? Wasn't his suicidal depression presaged in his despairing painting *Crows over the Wheatfield* in 1890? And wasn't his depression rooted in the collapse of his religious belief when he broke with his family ten years earlier? And wasn't that earlier belief a form of aberrant, morbid fanaticism that he was well rid of—to gain the freedom, if not the peace, of his later nature religion?

If recent research is correct, the answer to each of these questions is no. Van Gogh scholarship itself has suffered from its own tone deafness, and a very different picture emerges when van Gogh's faith is taken seriously. Academic monographs may ignore his beliefs, but his correspondence abounds in biblical quotations, prayers, stories of his missionary work, and arguments over interpretations of faith. The Rijksmuseum in Amsterdam may keep some of his explicitly religious paintings in the vault—such as *The Pietà* and *The Raising of Lazarus*—but van Gogh himself discussed them much more than the paintings normally on view. Only by taking seriously his belief throughout his life can some of his more famous paintings, such as *Starry Night* and *The Sower*, be understood.

LIKE JESUS

As pointed out by Kathleen Powers Erickson, a recent biographer, Vincent van Gogh was deeply religious over all his life, not just in the explicitly missionary years between 1875 and 1880. So it's impossible to divide his life neatly between his "fanatical years" and his "nature religion" years. Besides, while he certainly rejected the church in 1880, it wasn't the faith that he repudiated but the hypocrisy of the clergy. In many ways he carried the heart of his faith with him even after leaving the church for good—including his devotion to Jesus, his respect for the Bible, his belief in the kingdom of God on earth, his concern for the poor, and his conviction that an afterlife would reward those who, like him, had suffered so much on earth.

But there's certainly a huge rift at the center of van Gogh's life, a sharp rupture whose devastating effects marked him to the end. Born in a family for whom religion and art were always closely related, Vincent van Gogh had a deep admiration for his pastor-father and for the Arminian (not Calvinist) commitment of his family heritage. This more mystical pietism was deepened immeasurably by his time in London and Paris, where he experienced an evangelical conversion and grew to love Thomas à Kempis's *Imitation of Christ,* John Bunyan's *Pilgrim's Progress,* and Charles Haddon Spurgeon's preaching.

Van Gogh's desire then was to follow in his father's steps, but as a lay-evangelist rather than a pastor. "In our family," he wrote to his brother, Theo, "there has always been, from generation to generation, someone who preached the Gospel." But his efforts were a miserable failure. Eighteen months' trial run as a missionary to Belgian coal miners and a turn at employment in the family art business both ended dismally.

Van Gogh was dismissed from his missionary position by a church committee, but not for lack of faith. It was for his lack of eloquence in preaching. In fact they commended him highly for "the admirable qualities he displays at a sickbed or with the injured, to the devotion of self-sacrificing spirit, of which he gives constant proof." Asked why he lived a life of such ascetic deprivation, he answered, "I am a friend of the poor, like Jesus was."

Van Gogh's break with the church was finalized by his mistrust of the two clergy he had once admired most—his Uncle Stricker and his father. Repelled by the hypocrisy he saw in each of them, he accused all clergy and the institutional church as a whole of "Pharisaism." But he did not repudiate faith. Indeed, he wrote to his brother, "God perhaps really begins when we say the word with which Multatuli finishes his 'Prayer of an Unbeliever': 'O God there is no God!' For me, that God of the clergymen is dead as a doornail. But am I an atheist for all that?"

Van Gogh vehemently insisted that he still believed in God. In another letter to Theo he wrote: "You must not be astonished when, even at the risk of your taking me for a fanatic, I tell you that in order to love, I think it absolutely necessary to believe in God (that does not mean that you should believe all the sermons of the clergymen)…. Far from it. To me, to believe in God is to feel that there is a God, not dead or stuffed, but alive, urging us toward steadfast love with irresistible force."

From then on, van Gogh expressed the dichotomy between "good" and "bad" religion, the *"rayon blanc"* and *"rayon noir"* (white light and black light). "There really are," he wrote in another letter, "no more unbelieving and hard-hearted and worldly people than clergymen and especially clergymen's wives." His symbol for such hypocrisy was "the whitewashed wall." He said of the church, "No wonder one becomes hardened there and turns to stone."

TO HEAVEN ON FOOT

Revealingly, when van Gogh painted *Starry Night,* the whitewashed church is the only building in the landscape that does not reflect the brilliance of the stars above. The church alone is dark, but the sky is ablaze with light and faith. Remarking on this work, he spoke of "having a terrible need of—shall I say the word—religion." At such times, he said, "I go out at night to paint the stars." He wrote to Theo in 1882 about the birth of a friend's child: "At such a moment one feels His presence—which is the same as saying, and I readily give this sincere profession of faith, I believe in God."

Paul Gauguin, his friend and fellow artist, wrote of van Gogh that "his Dutch brain was afire with the Bible." Perhaps the most powerful and moving witness to van Gogh's faith in his final years was his 1882 lithograph *At Eternity's Gate*, repeated in oil on canvas in 1890 as he recuperated at the asylum at St. Rémy, Provence. An old, bald man sits huddled over in a chair with his clenched fists pressed into his eyes. Surely, we think, it represents only the anguish, grief, and relentless hard lot of the poor. But no, the painter said, the peasant—like van Gogh himself—clings to faith even there: "There is something noble, something great, which cannot be destined for the worms.... This is far from all theology, simply the fact that the poorest little woodcutter or peasant on the hearth or miner can have moments of emotion and inspiration that give him a feeling of an eternal home, and of being close to it."

"We are pilgrims," van Gogh said in his one surviving sermon, "our life is a long walk or journey from earth to heaven." The journey motif recurs right through to the end of his life. "I always feel I am a traveler, going somewhere and to some destination," he wrote from Arles. "I know nothing about it, but it is just the feeling of not knowing that makes the real life we are living now like a one-way journey on a train."

So death, and even suicide, are not the end to one who believed in "the eternal home." We cannot get to a star while we're alive, van

Gogh argued, any more than we can take the train while we're dead. "So to me it seems possible that cholera, tuberculosis, and cancer are the celestial means of locomotion, just as steamboats, buses, and trains are terrestrial means. To die quietly of old age would be to go there on foot."

Sadly, van Gogh decided it was too slow to "go there on foot." But when his friends surrounded his body with all his unsold canvases, covered his coffin with a profusion of his favorite yellow flowers, and hung over his casket his *Pietà* with its red-haired, Vincent-like Jesus in transition from death to resurrection life, they expressed his unquenchable faith. "Much strife must be striven," he had said, "much suffering must be suffered, much prayer must be prayed, and then the end will be peace."

Van Gogh's wrenching story rivals Nietzsche's for its pain and loneliness. But the painter's faith-despite-everything stands in stark contrast with Nietzsche's atheism. Van Gogh believed to the end, despite solid reasons not to believe, whereas Nietzsche never once investigated the evidence for the Christian faith he attacked so vehemently and said explicitly that he'd had no bad experiences of Christians or the church. "If I wage war on Christianity," he wrote in *Ecce Homo*, "I have a right to do so, because I have never experienced anything disagreeable or frustrating from that direction—the most serious Christians have always been well disposed toward me."

Which raises a critical question for seekers: What sort of evidence truly counts as a contradiction of faith? More particularly, we'll examine two perceived roadblocks to faith that really aren't—two seemingly unanswerable objections to faith that, on closer inspection, open the door to a deeper, more rational faith. One roadblock is the skepticism born of old wounds, mainly psychological in origin. The other is the skepticism born of bad experiences inflicted by people of faith. Both roadblocks are highly understandable, but as we shall see, they sidestep the question of truth. In fact, closer examination reveals that in both cases philosophy is reduced to biography, and the rational argument has been replaced by an *ad hominem* argument—instead of considering the evidence for a belief, there's simply an attack on the person presenting the evidence.

ONLY A PROJECTION?

Why did van Gogh cling to faith so doggedly and Nietzsche oppose faith so vehemently and so totally? The answer leads us into the deadliest assault on religion in the modern world—the theory of projection—which on inspection turns out to act like a boomerang that comes back to hit the unsuspecting attacker.

The idea that religious belief is a projection or a form of wish fulfillment, and therefore an illusion, was launched by the philosopher Ludwig Feuerbach in the early nineteenth century, then given its most powerful statement by Sigmund Freud in *The Future of an Illusion*. Religious beliefs, he said, are "illusions, fulfillments of the oldest, strongest, and most urgent wishes of mankind.... Thus the benevolent rule of a divine Providence allays our fears of the dangers of life."

For many years this view, backed by Freud's prestige and the authority of science, was taken as the ultimate debunking of any claims to truth by religious belief. If religion could be explained away by social and psychological factors—as Marx, Nietzsche, and Freud claimed—it was a waste of time to investigate whether religious beliefs were true.

Closer investigation, however, has left Freud's theory with its wings severely clipped. It has turned what's left of his theory back on himself and on all who rely on the projection theory as the central weapon in their arsenal against religion. Why the rethinking? Freud's projection theory is now acknowledged to be his own personal view and not a part of psychoanalysis or science. He himself admitted to a friend: "Let us be quite clear on the point that the views expressed in my book form no part of analytic theory. They are my personal views."

Freud gives no evidence of basing his theory on empirical evidence. In fact, the founder of psychoanalysis had astonishingly little experience either in probing the psychology of belief in God or in caring for patients who were religious. Professor Paul Vitz of New York University examined Freud's entire work and concluded bluntly: "Nowhere did Freud publish a psychoanalysis of the belief in God based on clinical evidence provided by a believing patient. He never presented publicly any serious psychological evidence for his projection theory or for his other ideas about religion."

Since Freud's time, research has overwhelmingly contradicted the idea that religious belief is neurotic and destructive. Religious life, in fact, has been demonstrated to go hand in hand with better physical health, greater psychological well-being, and a generally positive social influence.

Even more astonishing, Freud's theory has been shown to provide a better explanation for atheism than for religious belief. Freud had written of "the intimate connection between the father complex and belief in God," and stated how psychoanalysis shows "that the personal god is logically nothing but an exalted father, and daily demonstrates to us how youthful persons lose their religious beliefs as soon as the authority of the father breaks down." He indicated that "an atheist's disappointment in and resentment of his own father unconsciously justifies his rejection of God."

This last point is particularly noted by Paul Vitz in his book *Faith of the Fatherless*. Exploring Freud's claim, Vitz examined the childhood of the most famous and intense atheists—Nietzsche, Hume, Russell, Hitler, Stalin, Mao Zedong, Sartre, Camus, Schopenhauer, Madalyn Murray O'Hair, and others—and concluded, "We find a weak, dead, or abusive father in every case." For some, their fathers died when they were very young (Nietzsche was four years old). Others had fathers who were emotionally remote or abusive.

In many of the cases Vitz studied, the link between atheism and a defective father was acknowledged openly, either by the atheist or by his family. H. G. Wells, whose mother was virtually abandoned by his cricket-playing father, wrote in his autobiography of the effect this had on his mother's faith: "Once she had dreamt of reciprocated love and a sedulously attentive God, but there was indeed no more reassurance for her except in dreamland. My father was at cricket, and I think she realized more and more acutely as the years dragged on without material alleviation, that Our Father and Our Lord, on whom to begin with she had perhaps counted unduly, were also away—playing perhaps at their own sort of cricket in some remote corner of the starry universe."

By turning back the projection theory on its proponents, am I arguing that atheism is untrue? Not at all. That's a separate question. The theory of projection is actually a modern turning on its head of the ancient biblical view of idolatry—idols in the Hebrew view are "nothings" projected onto the universe. So returning the compliment is fair game, but that game could go back and forth forever.

What I'm underscoring here is the need for discussing truth and evidence that this sort of atheism typically circumvents. It's clear that when the discussion is followed through to the end, two things emerge starkly: The atheists' dismissal of religious belief through projection theory is irrational in ignoring the question of evidence entirely (as Nietzsche admits in *Ecce Homo,* "I have absolutely no knowledge of atheism as an outcome of reasoning, still less as an event; with me it is obviously by instinct"), and it is *ad hominem* in attacking the person presenting the evidence.

CHILLY AND CRUEL

I said earlier that although philosophy is rooted in biography, it is more than biography. In the lives of many of these leading atheists, however, philosophy is virtually reduced to biography. To put it more carefully, biography has become all-decisive for their atheism, with remarkably little of a wider rational grounding. In Nietzsche's case, the roots are simple; he has no wider grievance than the absence through death of the father he had adored and idolized but later came to see as weak. In other cases, the roots are more complicated, which leads to the second type of objection—skepticism because of bad experiences inflicted by people of faith.

Samuel Butler hated his father, who was both a tyrant and a clergyman. He therefore revolted against both his father's beatings and his faith. Not only did he lack a generally positive image of a father, he had a very particularly negative experience of his real father. The resulting hatred infected all his writing. Malcolm Muggeridge, his biographer, remarked: "There is hate in every reference Butler makes to his childhood. He came to see that words were like poisoned darts that he could plunge into the breasts of his enemies…and bring his father's church, his father's God, his father's hopes and beliefs and standards of behavior tumbling down one after another."

Experiences of weak, abusive, or absent fathering could be related endlessly, even among people whose faith survived. To Emily Dickinson, God was often as chilly, taciturn, and austere as her lawyer-father. When a friend asked about her family, she described her father as being "too busy with his Briefs—to notice what we do." She considered the deity he worshiped to be equally remote, saying of her family, "They are religious—except me—and address an Eclipse every morning—whom they call their 'Father.'"

These stories highlight a point that goes far beyond defective fatherhood: Over the course of two thousand years, there has consistently been one unanswerable objection to the Christian faith—Christians. Clearly there's a direct link between one's profession of faith, one's practice of faith, and the plausibility of that faith to others. Practice what you preach and you commend your faith; don't and you contradict it. "By this all men will know you are my disciple," Jesus said to his followers, "if you love one another." Or as Erasmus reminded his contemporaries in more corrupt times a millennium and a half later, "If we would bring the Turks to Christianity, we must first be Christians."

Sometimes the point has been expressed tartly—"Christianity might be a good thing," George Bernard Shaw quipped, "if anyone ever tried it"—and sometimes sadly, as in Archbishop William Temple's remark: "'I believe in the Holy Catholic Church,' and I only regret it does not exist." But the point is a momentous one for serious seekers. With a history that includes Richard Coeur de Lion's massacres in the Crusades, Torquemada's burning of Jews and heretics in the Spanish Inquisition, and the malignant pornocracy of the Borgia pope, Alexander VI, the case for the Christian faith must always be made with confession and humility.

Numerous counterarguments could and have been made—that no faith is responsible for its followers or that these evils have been inflated out of proportion. If ten thousand people died in the fires of the Inquisition, that fact should be weighed, some argue, against the more than one hundred million slaughtered under atheistic ideologies in the twentieth century. And so on.

But all such defenses miss the point. Whether the atrocity was committed against one, ten, two hundred, or ten thousand, it was still an atrocity. And nowhere more atrocious than in its flat-out contravention of the example and teaching of the one in whose name the atrocities were committed. In short, there's no getting around the necessity for confession. As C. S. Lewis acknowledged in a plea to his fellow Christians: "If ever the book which I am not going to write is written, it must be the full confession by Christendom to Christendom's specific contribution to the sum of human cruelty. Large areas of the world will not hear us until we have publicly disowned much of our past. Why should they? We have shouted the name of Christ and enacted the service of Molech."

STILL THIRSTY FOR TRUTH

But does this evidence count against faith? As we noted earlier, Camus underscored that beliefs should be judged by their peaks, not their by-products. The point seems especially valid when the actions of Christians so plainly and totally contradict the teachings and example of Christ.

And if such contradictions mean that the believer must be humble, the record of a false use of those contradictions means also that the skeptic must be honest. The decisive question is not whether believers fall short of their beliefs but whether those beliefs are true. Old wounds and bad experiences are a sad and inescapable reality in all religions and ideologies, but they aren't by themselves a reason to believe or disbelieve.

In her quest for meaning, Anne Lamott was forced to admit, "No one in our family believed in God—it was like we'd all signed some sort of loyalty oath early on, agreeing not to believe in God in deference to the pain of my father's cold Christian childhood." Was this rational? Had she looked at the truth of the matter? Plainly the answer in both cases was no. Her father's reaction to her grandparents' failures was no excuse. It was time to search seriously for herself, and this she did. "I was thirsty for something," she wrote, "that I will dare to call the truth."

———————

Do you have grounds for instantly dismissing a faith that you've never examined yourself? Are your attitudes toward faith colored by history or the experiences of your own life? Where are your attitudes rational? Where are they purely personal? Where are they inherited? Where are they merely a smoke screen?

Let your heart and mind run deep. Look closely at the confirmations and disconfirmations on the long journey home.

CHAPTER THIRTEEN

A PERFECT FIT

"Bless you, prison!" was Aleksandr Solzhenitsyn's famous exclamation about the infamous Gulag Archipelago. "I hate to think what sort of writer I would have become," he wrote in *The Oak and the Calf*, "if I had not been *put inside*."

Solzhenitsyn's "blessing" rings out far beyond his own indebtedness to imprisonment. Many of the world's great writings were conceived or written behind prison bars, from the prison letters of St. Paul to Boethius's *Consolation of Philosophy* to John Bunyan's *Pilgrim's Progress* to Dietrich Bonhoeffer's *Letters and Papers from Prison* to Vaclav Havel's *Letters to Olga*, as well as Solzhenitsyn's works. Some of the writers, such as Boethius and Bonhoeffer, actually wrote under sentence of death and were then executed.

For Martin Luther King Jr., the prison sentence was short—nine days—and so was the product, his twenty-page "Letter from Birmingham Jail." A blend of Old Testament justice and New Testament grace, and a prophetic message of America's civil rights movement, the letter is a highly acclaimed testament to the reforming passion of the man of faith who wrote it and to the vision of faith that inspires and directs such reform. But first reactions were far from universally positive.

A UNIVERSAL VOICE

In the spring of 1963 the civil rights movement was pushing for increased black voter registration across the South. At first the national spotlight fell not on King's efforts in Birmingham, Alabama, but on the initiatives of Bob Moses in Greenwood, Mississippi, where comedian Dick Gregory was the first national celebrity to offer help. "We will march through your dogs!" Gregory had said in a well-publicized speech. "And if you get some elephants, we'll march through them. And bring on your tigers and we'll march through them."

In Birmingham, "the Bastille of segregation," the protests planned by King—who was gaining the reputation of "a reluctant and losing crusader"—were criticized even by many sympathizers. The city's mayor-elect was planning reforms, and he urged "everyone, white and Negro, calmly to ignore" the protests. Attorney General Robert F. Kennedy described the demonstrations as "ill-timed."

A city injunction against protesting put King between a rock and a hard place. If he led the protests as he had promised, he would be leading many to jail, knowing that the movement no longer had the money to bail them out. Even King's father urged his son to obey the city's injunction. But King told his comrades, "I have to go. I am going to march if I have to march by myself."

King led the march on Good Friday and was promptly arrested by Birmingham police and placed in solitary confinement. From newspapers and magazines smuggled into the cell, King sadly noted the reaction to his march. *Time* called his stand "a poorly timed protest."

A PERFECT FIT

The *Washington Post* attacked it as one of "doubtful utility" sparked more by leadership rivalries than by real needs in Birmingham. Especially troubling was an item in the *Birmingham News* titled "White Clergymen Urge Local Negroes to Withdraw from Demonstrations." Liberal clergy, his former supporters, were questioning King's moral grounds for civil disobedience.

His response was the "Letter from Birmingham Jail." Stirred to the depth of his being, he sat down to scribble around the margins of the newspaper his reply to the religious leaders. His friend and lawyer, Clarence Jones, recalled the "jumble of biblical phrases wrapped around pest control ads and garden club news." His supporters deciphered and typed out King's scratchings, and the letter's audience in time would reach across the nation and around the world.

Written with white-hot intensity, the "Letter from Birmingham Jail" is remarkable by any standard. Some sentences are short and sharp, with a staccato sternness in their attack. Others are three hundred words long, like a flood of history and emotion carrying everything before it. Sometimes King's view expands to take in the perspective of millions; sometimes it contracts to see a single child at a particular moment. Sometimes he preaches, sometimes he pleads, sometimes he protests, sometimes he laments. Always he is passionate to persuade.

The letter revealed an "unassailable breadth" to the voice King projected, as historian Taylor Branch observed—"a kind of universal voice, beyond time, beyond race."

The letter included scathing attacks on white moderates, pithy pronouncements on the principles of justice, and more. "You express a great deal of anxiety over our willingness to break laws," he wrote to the clergy upset by his illegal protest in Birmingham. Their concern was legitimate, he admitted. He had urged people to obey the

Supreme Court's 1954 decision outlawing segregation in the public schools, and now his civil disobedience seemed paradoxical. "One may well ask: 'How can you advocate keeping some laws and breaking others?'"

King's response went to the heart of the view of reform made possible by the biblical faiths. "The answer lies in the fact that there are two types of laws: just and unjust. I agree with St. Augustine that 'an unjust law is no law at all.'"

An example of an unjust law, he noted, was one that deprived citizens of what was otherwise legally and morally right, as when Birmingham's ban on protests was used "to maintain segregation and to deny citizens the First Amendment privilege of peaceful assembly and protest." There was a right way to break such laws: "One who breaks an unjust law must do so *openly, lovingly,* and with a willingness to accept the penalty." Such a lawbreaker is not evading law, but giving a bigger picture, a wider portrayal of law: "I submit that an individual who breaks a law that conscience tells him is unjust and who willingly accepts the penalty of imprisonment in order to arouse the conscience of the community over its injustice is in reality expressing the highest respect for law."

Behind King's words are the same tensions we saw earlier in the bifocal vision of the biblical family of faiths—but with an important new application. The dynamic tension between the truth of creation and the truth of the fall that makes the biblical faiths both world-affirming and world-denying also carries a built-in impulse to reform. Wherever human injustice comes up short in contrast to divine justice, the challenge to remedy and rectify is not only permissible but required. "Am I not a man and a brother?"—this question on behalf of slaves was asked by William Wilberforce and Josiah Wedgwood to awaken Europeans to the evil of chattel slavery. "All segregation statutes are unjust," cried King in his letter, "because segregation distorts the soul and damages the personality."

IF THE FACTS WON'T FIT

Unquestionably this bifocal vision makes a difference. Faced with a world gone awry, the Hindu, for example, seeks to renounce it, whereas the Jew and the Christian seek to reform it. No one can look at their respective civilizations and fail to notice the consequences. But is this bifocal vision true?

There are two equal and opposite mistakes people make in answer to this question. Some people set up impossible standards for truth that no one could pass. Before anything can be accepted as true, they say, it must be tested. But how do we test the test to know that it establishes truth? We need another test. The desired certainty dissolves into circularity. The rationalist who sets out as an optimist in search of certainty ends up a pessimist and a skeptic.

On the other hand, other people simply bypass the question of truth altogether. With faith so illuminating and sustaining, who cares whether it's supported by evidence? Religious believers are commonly accused of being the chief culprits here, so much so that faith is often defined as "believing despite evidence." But there are also blatant secularist examples of such irrationality.

After Charles Darwin sent his brother a copy of *The Origin of Species,* his brother enthusiastically wrote back, saying natural selection was so compelling a theory that the lack of evidence at crucial points didn't trouble him. "In fact," he wrote, "if the facts won't fit in, why, so much the worse for the facts is my feeling."

Harvard biologist Richard Lewontin, writing in the *New York*

Review of Books, noted that because naturalistic scientists like himself "have a prior commitment...to materialism," they are willing to adopt certain positions in spite of common sense. "It is not that the methods of science somehow compel us to accept a material explanation of the phenomenal world," he wrote. On the contrary, "we are forced by our a priori adherence to material causes to create an apparatus of investigation and a set of concepts that produce material explanations, no matter how counterintuitive, no matter how mystifying to the uninitiated. Moreover, that materialism is absolute, for we cannot allow a Divine Foot in the door."

The leap of faith and the close-mindedness in these startling admissions are unmistakable. Clearly truth, evidence, openness, and investigation are not the principal considerations for such Darwinians.

In contrast, there are two ways we can investigate beliefs to see whether they fit with the evidence. Both are very important at this stage of the quest for meaning. One way, which is the subject of the next chapter, is to examine particular beliefs close up and in detail. The other, which we'll look at here, is to see the big picture—to assess large webs of interwoven truth claims that are the essence of a worldview. It means investigating various possible approaches to see which model is better at explaining the most facts.

Such assessments are prominent in science—and have resulted, for example, in the rejection of Ptolemy's earth-centered view of our immediate universe in favor of the sun-centered model advanced by Copernicus and Galileo. With the winning viewpoint now so well established, many forget that for centuries each view claimed to explain the facts better than the other. The victor was the model whose large-scale theories answered more questions and incorporated more facts than the other.

At Peace with the Universe,
at War with the World

Such a large-scale investigation of beliefs and world-views is, for many seekers, a key part of their quest, and always a unique one. After G. K. Chesterton was turned into a seeker by the sense of gratitude exploding in his mind, his ensuing search was distinctively his own (as is true for us all). His questions were not Augustine's or Pascal's or C. S. Lewis's or yours or mine. And he posed his distinctive questions to every faith he investigated.

In particular, Chesterton wanted to know why he experienced the world as good and bad *simultaneously*. Pessimism by itself did not satisfy him; he was genuinely grateful to be alive. But optimism by itself didn't satisfy him either; there was something profoundly amiss with the world. An acceptable faith would have to do justice equally to both parts of his experience of reality.

You can imagine Chesterton's excitement when it hit him that the Christian faith was criticized for bringing together the very two things he was trying to combine. "Christianity was accused, at one and the same time, of being too optimistic about the universe and too pessimistic about the world. The coincidence made me suddenly stand still."

The reason, Chesterton realized, lay in this bifocal vision encompassing the twin truths of creation and fall, giving the biblical faiths the "blessedly two-edged character" that C. S. Lewis noted later. Chesterton was transfixed. If this was true, it would solve his dilemma. "In this way at least one could be both happy and indignant without degrading oneself to be either a pessimist or an optimist. On this system one could fight all the forces of existence without deserting the flag of this world. One could be at peace with the universe and yet be at war with the world."

Chesterton's excitement mounted until there came for him a sudden daybreak, "an experience impossible to describe," as he later wrote about in *Orthodoxy:* "It was as if I had been blundering about since my birth with two huge and unmanageable machines, of different shapes and without apparent connection—the world and the Christian tradition." On the one hand he observed "this hole in the world, the fact that one must somehow find a way of loving the world without trusting it; somehow one must love the world without being worldly." On the other he found "this projecting feature of Christian theology, like a sort of hard spike, the dogmatic insistence that God was personal, and had made a world separate from Himself." This "spike of dogma," he discovered, "fitted exactly into the hole in the world—it had evidently been meant to go there."

"And then," Chesterton wrote, "the strange thing began to happen. When once these two parts of the two machines had come together, one after another, all the other parts fitted and fell in with an eerie exactitude. I could hear bolt after bolt over all the machine falling into its place with a kind of click of relief. Having got one part right, all the other parts were repeating that rectitude, as clock after clock strikes noon. Instinct after instinct was answered by doctrine after doctrine."

Varying the picture, Chesterton said he felt like a general advancing into hostile country to take a strategic fortress, only to find the whole country surrendering and falling into line. With these core truths in place, everything else fell into place and his life made sense. He felt the relief, he said, of "when a bone is put back into the socket." These Christian truths simply fitted, and he felt both the ease and the exhilaration of finding the fit.

The enjoyment of life that Chesterton had called his "haunting instinct" had found its reason. He had been led unerringly by the signal of transcendence that bleeped in his gratitude to be alive. His innate optimism had discovered a foundation strong enough to hold up even his outsized ebullience. And the reason for that optimism had been reversed and deepened. "I had often called myself an optimist," he explained, "to avoid the too evident blasphemy of pessimism. But all the optimism of the age had been false and disheartening for this reason, that it had always been trying to prove that we fit into this world. The Christian optimism is based on the fact that we do *not* fit in to the world."

He had found the pleasure promised by this false optimism of naturalism to be merely "prosaic," while "the Christian pleasure was poetic, for it dwelt on the unnaturalness of everything in the light of the supernatural." The discovery of a true "unnaturalness" had an astounding effect. "The modern philosopher had told me again and again that I was in the right place, and I had still felt depressed even in acquiescence." But after hearing "that I was in the *wrong* place...my soul sang for joy, like a bird in spring. The knowledge found out and illuminated forgotten chambers in the dark house of infancy. I knew now why grass had always seemed to me as queer as the green beard of a giant, and why I could feel homesick at home."

ACCUMULATION OF FACTS

Have you ever felt this *both-and* insistence to weld your optimism and pessimism together? Many have. "Man is neither angel nor beast," Pascal wrote, "and it is unfortunately the case that anyone trying to act the angel acts the beast." "Actually it seems to me," C. S. Lewis wrote to a friend, "that one can hardly say anything either bad enough or good enough about life." "Man is that being," wrote Viktor Frankl, "who invented the gas chambers of Auschwitz; however, he is also that being who entered those chambers upright, with the Lord's prayer or the *Shema Yisrael* on his lips."

The *both-and* insistence at the heart of Chesterton's discovery was an intellectual confirmation as well as a personal discovery. "If I am asked, as a purely intellectual question, why I believe in Christianity, I can only answer...I believe in it quite rationally upon the evidence. But the evidence in my case...is not really this or that alleged demonstration; it is in an enormous accumulation of small but unanimous facts." His faith now corresponded perfectly to the big picture he saw.

The Christian faith gave Chesterton an optimism with a difference, a pessimism with a difference, and a justification for both at the same time. And in the process, he found it to be true in a way that became the foundation for his journey through life and beyond.

———

Do you have an answer to why we're never fully at home in the world? And why we feel "homesick at home" with longings that soar beyond life?

Do you have an answer to why we feel the world should have been otherwise? And why "injustice anywhere is a threat to justice everywhere"?

Do you see a faith that answers all these questions and more?

Let your heart and mind run deep. Look closely at the confirmations and disconfirmations on the long journey home.

THE BEST NEWS EVER

There is an old saying that there are two things no one can look at in the eye and not go mad—the glory of God and the evil of humanity. If ever a century confirmed the second half of this proposition, it was the twentieth. With more than a hundred million killed in war, another hundred million slaughtered in political repression, and countless millions slain in ethnic and sectarian conflicts, the twentieth century was the most murderous and one of the most evil centuries in all history. It only deepened the fact Ambrose Bierce bitterly observed in the previous century after the carnage of the American Civil War: "The defining feature of humanity is inhumanity."

Two recurring lessons from the evil in humanity's dark story of inhumanity are a surprise to many. First, evil hardens the heart to the point of tearlessness, and it takes goodness to crack the heart open. Second, under dire circumstances of suffering, which might be thought to wound or weaken faith in God, faith emerges stronger on the other side of hell on earth. In fact, as Viktor Frankl declared with the authority of a death-camp survivor, "The truth is that among those who went through the experience of Auschwitz, the number of those whose religious life was deepened—in spite, not to say because, of this experience—by far exceeds the number of those who gave up their faith."

The two lessons, of course, are linked. What becomes startlingly clear in the midst of evil's mystery is that the mystery of good is deeper and more powerful still. To encounter heart-cracking goodness in the very furnace of evil's affliction is to find a supreme impetus toward faith. This impetus is clearly visible in the story of what Philip Hallie discovered about a place called Le Chambon.

FROM TEARLESSNESS TO TEARS

If Auschwitz and the other concentration camps were the midnight hour of human evil in the twentieth century, most responses at the time were an exercise in turning a blind eye and passing by on the other side of the street. Among the rare beacons of light were the extraordinarily courageous citizens of Le Chambon-sur-Lignon, a town of three thousand in German-occupied southern France. These brave townspeople, Huguenots who themselves had been persecuted for four hundred years, sheltered and saved more than five thousand Jewish children otherwise bound for the death camps.

Philip Hallie, a professor of philosophy and himself a Jew, did not know of Le Chambon for some time, even though he fought in World War II and his later studies led him deep into the darkness of the Nazi death camps and their perpetrators. His special interest was institutionalized cruelty, and as he delved deeper and deeper into the subject he felt himself becoming a victim too. "I was trying to be 'objective' about my studies," he wrote later, "when I was succeeding in being indifferent to both the victimizers and the victims of these cruel relationships. I became cold; I became another monster who could look upon the maiming of a child with an indifferent eye."

Then one day in 1975, during a period of near-suicidal depression, Hallie came across a short article on a little village in the Haute-Loire, in the mountains of southern France. As usual, he was reading the pages with an eye to objectivity, trying to sort out one more incident of cruelty and resistance to it. "About halfway down the third page of the account of this village," he later recalled, "I was annoyed by a strange sensation on my cheeks. The story was so simple and so factual that I had found it easy to concentrate upon *it*, not upon my own feelings. And so, still following the story, and thinking about how neatly some of it fit into the old patterns of persecution, I reached up to my cheek to wipe away a bit of dust, and I felt tears upon my fingertips. Not one or two drops; my whole cheek was wet."

Those tears, Hallie wrote, were "an expression of moral praise." Or as he explained in a later introduction to his account of Le Chambon, *Lest Innocent Blood Be Shed,* "one of the reasons I wept at the first reading about Le Chambon in those brief, inaccurate pages, was that I had discovered an embodiment of goodness in opposition to cruelty. I had discovered in the flesh and blood of history, in people with definite names in a definite place at a definite time in the nightmare of history, what no classical or religious ethicist could deny was goodness."

Hallie later went further. In a talk he gave in Minneapolis to a group of fund-raisers for the United Jewish Appeal, he mentioned the story of Le Chambon. After the talk, a woman stood up and asked, with a marked French accent, if he was referring to Le Chambon in the Haute-Loire (there are several French villages by the same name). He was, Hallie answered. After a pregnant silence, she continued, "Well, you have been speaking about the village that saved the lives of all three of my children."

After thanking Hallie for his book, she came to the front of the room to face the audience. "The Holocaust was storm, lightning, thunder, wind, rain, yes," she said. "And Le Chambon was the rainbow."

Several in the room gasped. As Jews, they understood her well. As Hallie commented, "We understood that the rainbow is one of the richest images in the Bible.... The rainbow reminds God and man that life is precious to God, that God offers not sentimental hope, but a promise that living will have the last word, not killing."

As he heard this woman from Minneapolis witnessing to such hope, Hallie realized "that for me too the little story of Le Chambon is grander and more beautiful than the bloody war that stopped Hitler." Indeed, he said, "The story of Le Chambon gives me an unsullied joy.... It has something supernatural in it."

Le Chambon was a place "where help came from love, not force," he wrote. And in a sense, Hallie himself was one of the Jews rescued by the Chambonais, although for him it came thirty years after the war was over.

EVIL AS A WAY TO GOD?

Philip Hallie was among several distinguished philosophers for whom evil has been the gateway, not the barrier, to faith. Another is Eleonore Stump, whose story of coming to God is told in her recent autobiographical essay, *The Mirror of Evil.* After noting hideous examples of suffering taken from the morning newspaper, she wrote: "This evil is a mirror for us. It shows us our world; it also shows us ourselves.... We ourselves—you and I, that is—are members of the species that does such things." She enumerated different responses to this fact: Some

THE BEST NEWS EVER

people quickly look away; some can't shut out the sight; some labor at obliviousness; some become global reformers; some react with loathing—loathing at the world or loathing of themselves.

As an example of the "inability to look away from the loathsome horrors in the mirror of evil," she cited Philip Hallie and his studies of Nazi cruelty and used it to raise this question: How do we know that the torture of Jewish children by Nazi doctors is evil?

Stump's answer as a philosopher is not reason or memory or sense perception, but intuition: We have "a cognitive faculty that recognizes evil intuitively." We may not understand it rationally, but we rely on it and use it all the time. Moreover, this faculty can discern differences between "ordinary wrongdoing and real wickedness" and also recognizes the opposite of wickedness, which Stump called "true goodness."

And here, she said, is where tears come in. We become accustomed to evil and bad news until our hearts are so hardened that we don't mind the evil as much. "And then good news cracks your heart.... We sometimes weep when we are surprised by true goodness."

We may glimpse this true goodness in other people or in the beauty of nature or mathematics or music. "But I have come to believe," Stump wrote, "that ultimately all true goodness of the heartbreaking kind is God's."

Stump's conclusion flies in the face of the facile skepticism that sees all evil as contradicting God's existence: "So, in an odd sort of way, the mirror of evil can also lead us to God. A loathing focus on the evil of our world and ourselves prepares us to be the more startled by the taste of true goodness when we find it and the more determined to follow that taste until we see where it leads. And where it leads is to the truest goodness of all.... The mirror of evil becomes translucent, and we can see through it to the goodness of God. There are some people, then, and I count myself among them, for whom focus on evil constitutes a way to God."

TWISTS OF THE CORKSCREW

Eleonore Stump's conclusion is unassuming: "This is the best I can do to tell my story." But the approach she highlighted, one that she and Philip Hallie demonstrated so well, is central to the climax of the third stage in our quest for meaning: After looking at a world-view's broad-gauge, large-scale evidence, the seeker must go on to examine in close detail its keystone belief.

For the Christian faith, this keystone belief is the identity of Jesus of Nazareth. And contrary to widespread misconceptions, the surest way to explore that belief is to examine it as something fully factual and historical but also as something more—as evidence about a person whom countless millions have come to recognize—and therefore trust and worship—as the ultimate case of heart-cracking goodness in human form.

Who was, who is Jesus of Nazareth? Or, in his own provocative question near the climax of his three-year engagement with seekers, "Who do you say I am?" Having wrestled with this question in my own search and having accompanied others examining it, I often compare the process of examination to the movement of a corkscrew. In contrast to the straight cut of a knife, a corkscrew penetrates by spiraling down, deeper and deeper, until the stopper is out, the bottle is open, and the wine can flow.

The first twist of the corkscrew lies in exploring certain preliminary conclusions about Jesus that are incontrovertible two thousand years after his birth. By any standard, Jesus of Nazareth is the most influential and captivating figure in world history and the supreme figure in the civilization that is currently the world's most powerful as the bearer of democracy, capitalism, science, the universities, philanthropy, medicine, and human rights, each of which owes something to him. In fact, most of the best of the ideals and ideas of Western civilization have been inspired or mediated by the faith that worships God in his name.

From birth to death, from the family to the government, from personal names to holidays, from the arts to the sciences, and from schools and colleges to hospitals and voluntary associations, there is no corner of Western civilization into which the light of the influence of Jesus has not shone. Historian W. E. H. Lecky described the teaching of Jesus as "the most powerful moral lever that has ever been applied to the affairs of man."

But the faith that worships Jesus cannot be dismissed as being exclusively European or even Western. West Asian in origin, the Christian faith is the world's first truly universal religion. Its adherents, found on every continent, make up a third of the earth's population. The Christian church has accurately been described as the most diverse society on earth.

Yet it would be ludicrous to approach Jesus through a focus on history, civilization, and impact alone. For one thing, that lens has been distorted by the later history of Constantine and Christian triumphalism. For another, the real Jesus was consistently dismissive of the world's power and glory in his day, just as he would undoubtedly be dismissed by today's powers that be. Given his homeless lifestyle, he would be harassed and moved on by today's police in Europe. Given his teenaged mother's lack of a wedding ring, he would be an automatic candidate for abortion if conceived in America. And given his ancestry, he would certainly have been pinned with a yellow star and shipped to the nearest death camp had he lived in Germany in the 1930s.

Again we give the corkscrew a twist. Far from a matter of power and glory, the record of the real Jesus points to the mystery of his unlikely significance. No one has captured this other side of Jesus better than the old meditation, "One Solitary Life."

> He was born in an obscure village, the child of a peasant woman. He grew up in another village, where he worked in a carpenter shop until he was thirty. Then for three years he was an itinerant preacher. He never wrote a book. He never held an office He never had a family or owned a home. He didn't go to college. He never visited a big city. He never traveled two hundred miles from the place where he was born. He did none of the things that usually accompany greatness. He had no credentials but himself. He was only thirty-three when the tide of public opinion turned against him. He friends ran away. One of them denied him. He was turned over to his enemies and went through the mockery of a trial. He was nailed to a cross between two thieves. While he was dying…his execution- ers gambled for his garments, the only property he had on earth. When he was dead, he was laid in a borrowed grave through the pity of a friend.

A résumé like that is hardly the profile of a corporate executive, a Nobel Prize winner, or a presidential candidate—let alone Napoleon,

Julius Caesar, Alexander the Great, Genghis Khan, or any of the other great captains of history. And yet it is Jesus, rather than one of these captains, who is the central figure of the human race. "All the armies that ever marched," the meditation concludes, "all the navies that ever sailed, all the parliaments that ever sat, all the kings that ever reigned, have not affected the life of man on this earth as much as that one solitary life."

In *The Story of Civilization,* Will Durant noted succinctly the clear result in the grand showdown between the might of Rome—perhaps the greatest power of all time—and Jesus: "Caesar and Christ had met in the arena, and Christ had won." "O pale Galilean," the Roman emperor Julian said, "thou hast conquered." Even Napoleon acknowledged the superiority and sheer difference of Jesus: "Everything in Christ astonishes me. His spirit overawes me, and his will confounds me. Between him and whoever else in the world, there is no possible term of comparison. He is truly a being by himself.... I search in vain in history to find the similar to Jesus Christ, or anything which can approach the gospel."

What is it that brings together these two seemingly irreconcilable pictures of Jesus—both powerless and the all-powerful? In reality, who was he? A great moral teacher and example? A nationalistic firebrand and failed Jewish revolutionary? A wild-eyed prophet with the gleam of an apocalyptic end of the world in his eye? A wandering, cynical preacher? A shrewd Galilean holy man? Or, as he claimed, somehow more—much, much more?

Such questions go far beyond the questions surrounding any other great figure in history. For in the case of Jesus, one possible answer to his identity is so explosive and life changing—or so preposterous and offensive—that no entirely cool appraisal will ever be possible.

SATISFYINGLY SOLID

Our exploration of Jesus bites deeper with another twist of the corkscrew. What does it say of him that his claims, if not true, are so outrageous that many who do not revere him revile him? And what does it say that there is no serious rival to his place as the most influential figure in history? As Dallas Willard responds to those put off by considering the supremacy of Jesus in history, "Who else do you have in mind?"

Since the thoughtful seeker's quest is for truth and its evidence, the path cannot bypass a factual and historical investigation of Jesus of Nazareth. Four considerations are helpful in sorting through the confusion at this point.

First, the Christian view of Jesus at the heart of the Christian faith asks for no special pleading; it has to be investigated and checked out like any other claim to truth. No one should make a leap of faith and "just believe anyway."

Second, the best way to investigate the identity of Jesus is simply to examine the evidence of history; the problem with false views is not that they offend, but that they're fiction.

Third, the best way to investigate the historical evidence for Jesus is through a double approach—working forward from the expectations of first-century Judaism and backward from the evidence of the four gospels.

Fourth, conclusions that claim to answer the question "Who was Jesus?" must show that they deal satisfactorily with a trio of core historical issues: How did Jesus understand himself? Why did Jesus die? And what explains the explosive rise of the Christian church (a question that cannot be answered without considering the universal and early claims that Jesus rose from death)? For each, the evidence must be examined.

THE BEST NEWS EVER

For all three questions, a startling pattern of conclusions emerges from the facts. The situation is not, as often claimed, that modern questions have arisen to awkwardly challenge the serenity of a long-unchallenged orthodoxy. Rather, the long-held orthodox conclusion is the only one that does full justice to the wide range of extraordinary and sometimes puzzling historical evidence.

C. S. Lewis's approach to this evidence, as encountered in his own search, has become classic. His disbelief had been jolted sharply when a militant Oxford atheist had sat in his room at Magdalen College and remarked that the historical authenticity of the Gospels was remarkably solid. Solid? Possibly true? Lewis was disturbed because he immediately saw the implications. His honesty propelled him forward, particularly after reading G. K. Chesterton's discussion of the issue in *Everlasting Man*.

"What are we to make of Jesus Christ?" Lewis asked. The historical problem, as he saw it, was to reconcile two vital pieces of evidence about Jesus—the "depth and sanity of his moral teaching" on one hand, and "the quite appalling nature of this man's theological remarks" on the other.

Lewis was disturbed because all his reading and research made one conclusion unmistakably clear: No great moral teacher ever claimed to be God; in fact, the greater the teacher the less likely the claim. So what did it mean that, where Confucius, Buddha, Zoroaster, Socrates, and Muhammad all stopped short, the greatest teacher of all made this claim simply, straightforwardly, and repeatedly—and did so before his fellow Jews, the one people on earth absolutely predisposed to reject as blasphemy any notion that God could become man?

Lewis's fellow dons at Magdalen College, Oxford, were not serious in this discussion and were quite content to doff their caps to Jesus the great moral teacher while ignoring contrary evidence. But for Lewis, the literary historian, this wouldn't do. He had to be more rigorous. "Let us not come with any patronizing nonsense about his being a great moral teacher. He has not left that open to us. He did not intend to." The historical record showed both sides of the evidence, and Lewis knew there were only so many possible theories to explain the contradictions.

Perhaps Jesus of Nazareth was a liar. Perhaps he was a lunatic. Perhaps he was a legend concocted by his followers. Lewis weighed each possibility in turn and soberly rejected each on the basis of the evidence. Reluctantly, Lewis pursued the last remaining possibility: If Jesus spoke as God speaking through him, and acted as God acting in him, he was clearly speaking and acting *as God*. Jesus was speaking and acting as if he actually embodied the unthinkable—*Israel's God, YHWH, come down in person and in power*. If this was true, the only thing to do was to worship Jesus as Lord and God, as his first followers did.

SECOND-PERSON ENGAGEMENT

For many seekers, however, even the force of this logic isn't enough. It's still in the realm of a third-person account, impersonal and unconvincing. It takes another twist of the corkscrew that comes from a second-person engagement—a recognition that the factual and historical evidence for Jesus is inseparable from the personal mission of Jesus and the personal quest of the seeker. If anything in the four gospels is clear, it's that Jesus himself was on a search. He was seeking all who are out of touch with his father.

At this point, C. S. Lewis's approach has often been misused. It isn't a verbal party trick—liar, lunatic, legend, or Lord?—as if the question of "what are we to make of Jesus Christ?" could be considered and settled in as many seconds as it takes to say it. In itself the argument is only words on a page, and this clearly falls short. Instead, like a recipe, the argument has to be followed. Like a map, it has to be traveled. Like a conversation, it has to be engaged. After all, as the record of the Gospels shows, with all the manifold claims and evidence before their very eyes and ears, his earliest followers found the evidence so compelling, yet the enigma so mind-blowing, that the fastest of them took three years to reach their conclusion—which then turned their world upside down.

In the end, the purely factual is simultaneously all-important and unimportant. It's an essential part of faith, yet so small a part. The veteran Roman centurion put his trust in Jesus after discovering from his servants that at the very moment Jesus said his son would be well, his son recovered. The factual, the evidential, and the historical played a key part, but they were swallowed up and overwhelmed by the personal.

In a thousand ways, people who engaged with Jesus were stopped in their tracks by "the much, much more." His first followers responded to his call as an act of intuitive obedience long before they knew who he was. His teaching stunned audiences with its note of authority that belied his demographic background. His disciples reeled back amazed at the implications of his words stilling a storm. A woman caught red-handed in adultery was staggered to find herself protected rather than stoned. The two disciples walking on the road to Emmaus with the mysterious stranger found their hearts burning within them.

Each time the evidence about Jesus was there to be seen. The truth in one sense was unmistakable. But the first and last impression of those engaging with Jesus was of the much, much more. The ultimate goodness that cracked hearts open was speaking and acting in human form. In a myriad of individual ways, they came to recognize him with gratitude and wonder. Is it any surprise that what Jesus had announced as the "good news" of the arrival of God's rule on earth came to be the news specifically about Jesus himself? His followers came to see it as the decisive, definitive good news of all time—*the best news ever*.

Is it any surprise too that Jesus, the "man of sorrows" and "man for others," has had such a profound effect on the poor and suffering of the world—even on many outside the official orbit of his followers? Chaim Potok's Asher Lev witnessed to the deep effect of seeing Michelangelo's *Pietá* in the Duomo in Florence: "I was an observant Jew, yet that block of stone moved through me like a cry, like the call of seagulls over the morning surf—like the echoing blasts of the *shofar* sounded by the Rebbe. I do not mean to blaspheme. My frames of reference have been formed by the life I have lived. I do not know how a devout Christian reacts to that *Pietá*. I was only able to relate it to elements in my own lived past. I stared at it. I walked slowly around it. I do not remember how long I was there that first time. When I came back out into the brightness of the crowded square, I was astonished to discover that my eyes were wet."

TRUTH AND CHRIST

Perhaps this role played by heart-cracking goodness explains the mystery of Dostoevsky's famous *Credo*. Reaching out to a friend experiencing a time of deep dejection, Dostoevsky wrote to her that he himself was "a child of disbelief and doubt" and would remain so till the grave. "How much terrible torture this thirst for faith has cost me and costs me even now," he wrote, "which is all the stronger in my soul the more arguments I can find against it. And yet, God sends me sometimes instants when I am completely calm; at those instants I love and I feel loved by others, and it is at these instants that I have shaped for myself a *Credo* where everything is clear and sacred for me.

"This *Credo* is very simple," he continued. "Here it is: to believe that nothing is more beautiful, profound, sympathetic, reasonable, manly, and more perfect than Christ; and I tell myself with a jealous love not only that there *is* nothing but that there *cannot be* anything. Even more, if someone proved to me that Christ is outside the truth, and that *in reality* the truth were outside of Christ, then I should prefer to remain with Christ rather than with the truth."

Remain with Christ rather than with the truth? Are we back with the simplistic and the irrational? Is Dostoevsky betraying an atheism he wasn't honest enough to confess? Is the seeker being asked, at this late stage of the quest, to swallow a form of bad faith? Emphatically not! But with all the risk of Dostoevsky's reckless way of saying it, he was nailing his colors to the mast.

"Truth" and "Christ" are ultimately and absolutely indissoluble. Christ, after all, claimed to *be* the truth. And although truth and its evidence point to Christ, this is swallowed up by the fact that Christ is the ground and guarantee of truth—and also of freedom, joy, hope, love, and humanness itself. Ultimately, as Dostoevsky believed passionately, truth and humanness exist only if God exists. And no demonstration of God is clearer than Jesus.

Simone Weil, the French philosopher, later wrote of her own passionate search: "One can never wrestle enough with God if one do so out of pure regard for truth. Christ likes us to prefer the truth to him because, before being Christ, he is the truth. If one turns aside from him to go toward the truth, one will not go far before falling into his arms."

AN ENCIRCLING BLAZE

The world Jesus came to was reeling from the clash of empires and scarred by the tracks of conquering armies. It was ground down by poverty and cowed by the lash of injustice and suffering. Yet that old world was still fired by ancient dreams of justice and peace, so that into its tinder-dry longings the best news ever burst like a blaze. Now the blaze is encircling the earth.

For the first disciples in their time, for Dostoevsky in his, and for thoughtful seekers today, the truth about Jesus of Nazareth is there to be faced and examined and known in all its unvarnished facthood. But the confirmation of that truth comes from an engagement that passes through the factual to intuitive recognition of the personal. The evidence for Jesus is something to be sure of; recognizing what Jesus shows us of the heart-cracking goodness of God is something to be passionate about.

———

Who do you say Jesus is? Have you looked at the evidence yourself, or have you hidden behind the complexities of the controversies? What do you make of the incidents and claims that led people of all kinds to conclude that Jesus of Nazareth was not only a teacher and a prophet but more, so much more?

Let your heart and mind run deep. Look closely at the confirmations and disconfirmations on the long journey home.

PART FOUR

A TIME FOR COMMITMENT

CHAPTER FIFTEEN

NEVER MORE OURSELVES

◈

"We possess nothing in this world other than the power to say 'I.'" Simone Weil's words from the dark days before the Second World War are a cry that transcends the ages.

Unexpectedly, we may find ourselves confronting the cold threat of an incurable disease or a mugger's gun. We may suddenly be on the wrong side of an employer, a finance company, a divorce. More commonly, we may feel ourselves overwhelmed by the speed and scale of modern life. Yet in no situation do we lose the power to be ourselves. Even in reacting to situations beyond our control, we still can say "I."

TO PAY OR NOT TO PAY

Such responsibility must not be taken for granted. "The secret of man," Vaclav Havel wrote, "is the secret of his responsibility." The discovery of this secret is part and parcel of Havel's heroic rise to leadership of the Charter 77 movement that toppled the Soviets in

Czechoslovakia in 1989. The son of a civil engineer, Havel was thwarted for political reasons in gaining the higher education he sought, so he joined a Prague theater as a stagehand in the 1950s. Working his way up, he rose to become one of Europe's premier playwrights and used his growing voice on behalf of the emerging movement for human rights.

Author of many essays on the nature of totalitarianism, as well as a famous "Open Letter to Dr. Husak" (the Czech Communist leader) in 1975, Havel became a prime target for the regime. He was followed everywhere by the police and always carried with him an "emergency kit"—such things as toothpaste, cigarettes, and razor blades—in case he was arrested in the street.

The arrest finally came at five o'clock on the morning of May 29, 1979. Havel and fourteen other dissidents were sent to Ruzyne prison, where Havel was charged with "subversion." The nearly five years of imprisonment that followed gave Havel a chance for major reflection upon his life. He was allowed once a week to write to his wife, Olga, and used the occasion to express his profound thoughts on life and modern society. "True," he wrote, "I would rather be reading books of philosophy by real philosophers, but since that's impossible, my only recourse is to philosophize myself."

Published later as *Letters to Olga*, they are part personal and part philosophical, part description and part reflection. Havel's "testimony" to his "inner murmurings," as he calls them, covers a gamut of topics, but no theme recurs more strongly in the letters than human responsibility. "The tragedy of modern man," he wrote, " is not that he knows less and less about the meaning of his own life, but that it bothers him less and less."

He revealed how the topic was on his mind long before his prison sentence. "Dear Olga," he wrote in July 1982. "For many years now, whenever I have thought about responsibility or discussed it with someone, a trivial illustration has come to mind: At night, I board the rear car of a tram to go one stop. The car is empty, and since the fare is paid by dropping a crown into a box, not even a conductor is present.... So I have the option of throwing the fare into the box or not. If I don't no one will see me, or ever find out; no witnesses will ever be able to testify to my misdemeanor. So I'm faced with a great dilemma, regardless of how much money I happen to have with me: To pay or not to pay?"

That is the question, Havel says: When no one sees, to pay or not to pay? Like Plato's shepherd Gyges, who can do what he likes when he rubs his gold ring that makes him invisible, Havel saw the link between responsibility and invisibility. From an everyday point of view, it made no sense to pay the fare—a coin in the box "amounts to throwing it down the drain." Why then was he troubled by the choice? Certainly it wasn't because of consequences; since no one would ever know whether he paid or not, no one would ever commend or condemn him. Friends, fellow citizens, the transport commission, the state—all were absent and irrelevant to the issue. The conflict was entirely within himself. So why did something still urge him to pay? And why did the thought of not paying make him feel guilty?

Here, Havel reflected, was a conversation between his "I," with its freedom to choose and think about its choice, and something outside himself. But what was this "partner" in the dialogue, a partner we cannot see yet cannot escape or outwit? Some would say it's only conscience or an inner voice, but Havel thought not. It certainly addressed his conscience, but as something outside or higher.

"Who, then, is in fact conversing with me?" Obviously this something or someone was higher than the transport commission, his friends, and his immediate practical interests. Obviously, too, this partner was something or someone who is everywhere and knows everything, for the same challenges would arise wherever we are. "But who is it?" Havel asked. "God?"

Soon after writing this letter, Havel appeared before a prosecutor. On this occasion he felt he knuckled under to the Communists, and afterward he was deeply shaken and ashamed. In a subsequent letter he wrote, "I have my failure to thank for the fact that for the first time in my life I stood—if I may be allowed such a comparison—directly in the study of the Lord God himself: Never before had I looked into his face or heard his reproachful voice from such proximity, never had I stood before him with such profound embarrassment, so humiliated and confused, never before had I felt so deeply ashamed, or felt so powerfully how unseemly anything I could say in my own defence would be."

In the harsh glare of what he'd done, Havel was pushed beyond the link between responsibility and invisibility to see the even more challenging link between responsibility and identity. "By casting doubt on my own sense of responsibility, the shock I experienced, of course, cast doubt on my identity as well."

FULL PARTICIPATION

Havel's sense of being "in the study of the Lord God himself" is an apt illustration of the fourth stage in the quest for meaning—a time for commitment. Our conclusions come together and culminate in responsible action. Stepping forward, we can truly say that now we believe and now we've launched ourselves on our journey home to God.

A common mistake at this point is to allow the lure of technique to intrude again. Far too often the seeker is confronted by people who are out to simplify and "sell" the faith, reducing their understanding of it to a formula and promoting their method like a franchise. The effect can be to shrink the "great change" of conversion, as William Wilberforce called it. The commitment is reduced to a simplistic, stereotyped recipe that insults both the integrity and diversity of human beings and the sovereign freedom of God.

There are, as I said earlier, as many ways to faith as there are people who come to faith. Such variety is as true of this fourth stage as of all the others. Conversion may be gradual or sudden, quiet or dramatic, unmistakably obvious to others or virtually unnoticed. Such variations are infinite, but the reality of our experience is what matters.

Yet even in all the variety, a few pervasive themes stand out. One of them is the irreducible component of individual responsibility. Even if someone has grown up with the faith, it still must be chosen and entered into, not just inherited. Even if awareness of faith has crept in on silent feet like a dawn, the daylight reality of faith requires our full participation.

In the Christian faith, the good news of the gospel is a covenant agreement God offers to us through Jesus. It isn't enough for us to see only the need for what's offered (as we did in phase one) or even the attractiveness and reliability of the terms (as we did in phases two and three). The covenant becomes binding only when it is signed, and our signature is the binding declaration that each of us gives as a whole person.

There are obvious reasons why such a full commitment of faith is commonly diluted in the West today. With two thousand years of tradition, it easily becomes a formality. With purely theoretical understandings of knowledge common, it easily becomes abstract and remote. With loose and inadequate descriptions of faith in circulation, it easily becomes weak and irrational. For example, one of the commonest descriptions of faith—"a leap in the dark"—is also the faultiest, suggesting that faith is blind or not based on reason at all.

Kierkegaard popularized the term "leap of faith" in the nineteenth century. He used it to emphasize the passionate, personal, subjective nature of faith in contrast to the abstract Hegelianism of his day. But many who use the term now have toppled into an exaggerated irrationality that is equally extreme.

To avoid this irrationality, I prefer the term "step of faith" rather than "leap of faith." To be sure, the commitment of faith is more than reason—it is, after all, a whole person who makes the commitment, and whole people are more than walking minds. And yet faith is never less than rational. It is more than reason because we are whole people; it is never less than reason because, as we've seen in the first three stages, it is neither against reason nor lacking in reason. It is thoroughly rational yet also wholly personal.

THE WAY A LION KILLS

A thoughtful step of faith has three vital components. It includes *knowledge*, which grows into *conviction*, which grows into *trust*. Faith includes knowledge because we aren't asked to trust someone about whom we know nothing. It also includes conviction; we're not only attracted to what faith is about, but we have become sure of its truth.

And finally it includes trust, for having faith isn't merely being convinced of something; it is the entire person being committed to someone. For any follower of Jesus Christ who follows this path on the quest for meaning, the statement is true: *A Christian thinks in believing and believes in thinking.*

All of which has stunning consequences for our responsibility. Never in our lives are we freer, more active, and more responsible than when we act on the decision to put our faith in God and set out on the journey home to him. Never are we more ourselves.

A European recalled a conversation about faith with a Masai tribesman in Kenya. The European used a certain word to define the concept of belief, but the tribesman rejected his definition with a snort. The Masai word the European used simply meant "assent" or "agreement." The tribesman likened this inadequate word to "a white hunter shooting an animal with his gun from a great distance. Only his eyes and his fingers took part in the act."

But true belief, the tribesman said, could be pictured as a pursuing lion: "His nose and eyes and ears pick up the prey. His legs give him the speed to catch it. All the power in his body is involved in the terrible death leap and single blow to the neck with the front paw, the blow that actually kills. And as the animal goes down, the lion envelops it in his arms [Africans refer to the front legs of an animal as its arms], pulls it to himself, and makes it part of himself. This is the way a lion kills. This is the way a man believes. This is what faith is."

This full embrace of responsible faith is prominent in the climax of C. S. Lewis's journey from atheism to theism. What jolted him to begin his quest, as we saw, were the recurring experiences of being "surprised by joy." But as Lewis knew well, the point is to travel, not to marvel at the signposts. "When we are lost in the woods the sight of a signpost is a great matter," he wrote. "But when we have found the road and are passing signposts every few miles, we shall not stop and stare." The point is to hurry on to the destination.

As Lewis reached the threshold of faith, however, his mood changed again. Far from the stunned wonder of the atheist surprised by joy, or the disciplined earnestness of the seeker assessing possible answers, Lewis experienced a welter of confusion in the core of his being. "For the first time I examined myself with a seriously practical purpose. And there I found what appalled me; a zoo of lusts, a bedlam of ambitions, a nursery of fears, a harem of fondled hatreds. My name was legion."

He also experienced a strange challenge to decide. He knew he was being offered "a moment of wholly free choice." Sitting on the double-decker bus going up Headington Hill from Magdalen College to his home, he was aware that he was holding something at bay, shutting something out. What it felt like, he recalled, was that he was wearing stiff clothing, even a suit of armor, or that he was like a lobster in his protective shell. And throwing it off was entirely up to him: "I felt myself being, there and then, given a free choice. I could open the door or keep it shut; I could unbuckle the armor or keep it on. Neither choice was presented as a duty; no threat or promise was attached to either, though I knew that to open the door or to take off the corset meant the incalculable. The choice appeared to be momentous but it was also strangely unemotional. I was moved by no desires or fears. In a sense I was not moved by anything."

There on the bus, Lewis came to his decision. "I chose to open, to unbuckle, to loosen the rein. I say, 'I chose,' yet it did not really seem possible to do the opposite. On the other hand, I was aware of no motives. You could argue that I was not a free agent, but I am more inclined to think that this came nearer to being a perfectly free act than most that I have ever done."

"I am what I do," Lewis concluded. There's a moment when the choice to act moves beyond a discussion of motives, for even an awareness of our own motives can become a form of necessity that lets our responsibility off the hook. And the moment of faith is a moment when no part of us is excused. With no ifs, no buts, no conditions, no escape clauses, all we are is challenged to rise to the choice and shoulder the responsibility for our answer.

LAUNCH OUT INTO THE DEEP

This was certainly my own experience. There's a strong heritage of faith in my family, going back six generations to Arthur Guinness, the founder of our family brewing company and a man of strong faith. But that faith was neither close nor real to me. My parents were under house arrest by the Communists in China, and I was back at a boarding school in England. In a sense I found myself sheltered both from the Communists and from the possibility of any family faith that might either attract or repel.

I have always been an avid reader, especially of history and biography. The general thrust of my school was toward a classical English education, which I filled out with a rich diet of my own Continental reading—above all in Pascal, Kierkegaard, Dostoevsky, Nietzsche, Sartre, and Camus. The last three, I thought, had the better arguments. Of these, Albert Camus was my hero. I greatly preferred his warm humanity and passionate rebel's philosophy to the grandiosity of Nietzsche and the cold-fish intellectualism of Sartre.

What turned my thinking around was a combination of the wit and wisdom of G. K. Chesterton and C. S. Lewis and the power of the lives of my believing friends. Gradually the cracks and holes in the thought of Camus, Sartre, and Nietzsche became more visible, and the profundity of Pascal, Dostoevsky, Chesterton, and Lewis won the day.

But my search, although it had come hesitatingly close to a conviction of truth, still had an arm's-length quality about it. I knew my need. I was drawn to the power of the illumination of the answer. I could see the fit that demonstrated the truth of it all. But I was still at a safe distance from all this, detached and in control of my search.

That all changed one night when I heard a Scotsman open up the words (from the gospel of Luke) that Jesus spoke to his follower Peter: "Launch out into the deep." Like the rush of a powerful current out of nowhere, everything in my life changed suddenly as I listened. The distant loomed close. The blurred became clear. The faint became a roar. The motionless rose up before me as a living truth. I knew I was being addressed—I alone, without my friends, and in a way I could not duck if I was to be myself.

Launch out into the deep? At the mere word of Jesus? It was absurd. Peter knew that. He was the fisherman; Jesus was the rabbi. He would listen to Jesus all day and even lend him his boat from which to address the crowd. But fishing was something else. Fishing was his business, and he'd already fished fruitlessly that day. And yet. And yet.

The command that led to nets bursting with fish for Peter burned into my ears and spoke to my soul. Like the man in Franz Kafka's parable *He*, I knew I was on a path with the past pressing from behind, the future pressing from in front, and the present howling like a wind tunnel of forces. There was no escape and no alternative for me but to stand in the gap, to take my place on the gridiron of conflicts, and to make the choice that summoned up more of me than any choice in my life ever had. I bowed and committed myself without reservation to Jesus as Lord and have been on that venture ever since.

RESPONSIBLE FOR EVERY HOUR

Kierkegaard wrote that the significance of the Christian faith for society "ought to be to do everything to make every man eternally responsible for every hour he lives." The twin forces of diversion and bargaining make such responsibility unattainable, yet his point still stands, and it comes into its own in this fourth phase of the quest. We're never more ourselves than when we make the commitment that forms our part of faith. And the whole-person responsibility in that commitment marks the opening up of a life of growing responsibility.

"Who stands fast?" Dietrich Bonhoeffer asked in the dire days under the Nazis. "Only the man whose final standard is not his reason, his principles, his conscience, his freedom, or his virtue, but who is ready to sacrifice all this when he's called to obedient and responsible action in faith and in exclusive allegiance to God—the responsible man, who tries to make his whole life an answer to the question and call of God."

———

Are you ducking the questions that seeking raises to you? Is the quest still formal, abstract, and at arm's length for you? Or are you facing the challenge with all your heart, mind, and soul, rising to your full responsibility in answering all that God and life are addressing to you?

Let your heart and mind run deep. Engage with every fiber of your being on the long journey home.

THE HOUND
OF HEAVEN

When she was a student at the Sorbonne, they nicknamed her "the Red Virgin" because of her blend of radicalism and chastity. Her mind was so uncompromising that one of her professors called her "the categorical imperative in skirts." Another professor, who was her mentor and hero, called her "the Martian" because "she has nothing in common with us and sovereignly judged us all." One fellow student called her "undrinkable." Another wrote, "We had the impression that she came from somewhere else and had a thought-process that was not of our age or milieu."

Simone Weil has always provoked strong and paradoxical responses. To her friends and colleagues, her teachers, her biographers, and now her growing number of readers and admirers, she is so singular and angular that she strikes people as the personal equivalent of Churchill's comment on Russia: "a riddle wrapped in a mystery inside an enigma."

A SECULAR SAINT

Born in Paris in 1909 and dying a lonely death through tuberculosis and malnutrition in Ashford, Kent, in 1943, Simone Weil lived a short, sad, misunderstood life that on the outside appeared a failure and a waste. Yet she has been hailed since her death as the greatest spiritual thinker and one of the most astute political thinkers of her time. She was "the saint of all outsiders" to André Gide and a "secular saint" to Albert Camus, who wrote, "It is impossible to imagine a rebirth of Europe which does not take account of the requirements laid down by Simone Weil."

Weil has had her detractors too. They called her brilliant but arrogant, off-putting, masochistic. They said she made people uncomfortable. In her passionate commitment to truth and her unswerving insistence on suffering with the downtrodden, she was just too extreme, they said. She carried everything too far—including hastening her own death by virtually starving herself in solidarity with her fellow countrymen in wartime France.

And always there are the paradoxes. Weil was a combination of things that don't combine: She was a philosopher, she was an activist, she was a mystic. The daughter of a comfortable, middle-class family, she became an ardent champion of the working class. A declared Bolshevik at the age of ten, famous for her signature copy of the Communist paper *L'Humanité* in the pocket of her student overalls, she became one of the most stringent critics of Marxism. A fervent pacifist, she fought in the Spanish Civil War and joined the French Resistance movement and Charles de Gaulle's Free French. A lonely person, capable of writing on love with great beauty, she was repelled by any physical contact even with her friends. A Jew, she was devoted to Jesus and on the verge of baptism and acceptance into the Catholic Church, but she refused to take the step because of her surprising objection to how Christians saw themselves as heirs of the Old Testament. A realist to a fault yet one who never gave up hoping, Weil, in the description of David McLellan, her leading biographer, was a "utopian pessimist."

Some of Weil's admirers have tried to soften the paradoxes. They can be explained partly by the sharply distinct periods in her life (thinker, political activist, seeker, and mystic) or by the very different audiences to which she was writing (trade unionists, Catholic priests, Resistance leaders). But in the end the paradoxes won't go away—they remain a stubborn feature of her highly unusual personality and her passionate zigzag quest for meaning. Like George Orwell, Simone Weil will always be unsettling because she's finally unclassifiable and unclubbable.

There are, however, strong, consistent threads running through the twists and turns of Weil's life. For her seeker's quest, the two most vital were her passion for truth and her profound feeling for affliction, tied in with her inner certainty of a unique mission in life.

For Weil, affliction was more than suffering; it was a form of suffering that degraded and humiliated. When hired as an unskilled, female factory worker, she described it as having "received the mark of slavery." But she was determined to undergo the experience, especially since none of the great Communist leaders "had ever set foot inside a factory." Although claiming that "contact with affliction had killed my youth," her evident compassion for sufferers was both striking and appealing to others.

When the 1927 Sorbonne exam results were published, Simone de Beauvoir found all the men below her and only one person above her—Simone Weil. But it was Weil's compassion, not her brilliance, that stunned Sartre's future life companion. "A great famine had broken out in China, and I was told that when she had heard the news she had wept: those tears compelled my respect much more than her gifts as a philosopher. I envied her for having a heart that could beat right across the world."

Weil's fierce passion for truth was equally marked. In the 1920s and 1930s—decades filled with illusions, cant, insincerity, and demagoguery—she was intolerant of lazy thinking, white lies, and compromise of any kind. "In her presence," one classmate remembered, "all 'lies' were out of the question. But I also sometimes felt the need simply to escape from her denuding, tearing, and torn eyes which would swallow up and leave helpless the person she was looking at, transported against their will into the depths of Being."

Weil was no less severe on herself. "I didn't mind having no visible successes," she wrote in *Waiting for God,* "but what did grieve me was the idea of being excluded from that transcendent kingdom to which only the truly great has access and wherein truth abides. I preferred to die rather than live without that truth." Attaining truth was one reason she did not fear dying. The very moment of death was "the centre and object of life...the instant when, for an infinitesimal fraction of time, pure truth, naked, certain and eternal, enters the soul."

CHRIST CAME DOWN

Doubtless such drives fueled Weil's lifetime quest for meaning, although she was uncomfortable with much of the rhetoric of seeking. "It is not for man to seek, or even to believe in, God," she wrote in *On*

Science, Necessity, and the Love of God. "He has only to refuse his love to everything which is not God. This refusal does not presuppose any belief. It is enough to recognize, what is obvious to any mind, that all the goods of this world, past, present, or future, real or imaginary, are finite and limited and radically incapable of satisfying the desire which burns perpetually within us for an infinite and perfect good."

How did Simone Weil find satisfaction for that desire? Her journey was punctuated by a series of what she called "contacts with Catholicism that really counted." The first and gentlest came on a holiday in Portugal after her period of factory work, including a job at Renault. As she told it in *Waiting for God,* walking along a village beach, she came across a celebration of the feast of Our Lady of the Seven Sorrows. "Nothing can give any idea of it. I have never heard anything so poignant unless it were the song of the boatmen on the Volga. There the conviction was suddenly borne in upon me that Christianity is preeminently the religion of slaves, that slaves cannot help belonging to it, and I among others."

The second experience came in 1937 during two days Weil spent in Assisi. Alone in the twelfth-century chapel of Santa Maria degli Angeli, where St. Francis often used to pray, she encountered something that brought her nearer to faith, "something stronger than I was compelled me for the first time in my life to go down on my knees."

The third and climactic experience came during ten days Weil spent over Easter at the Benedictine abbey of Solesmes in northwestern France. The abbey was well known for the beauty of its plain chant, and she had gone there for aesthetic reasons. Racked by chronic violent headaches, she had taken to reflecting on George Herbert's seventeenth-century poem *Love,* to which she'd been introduced by a young Englishman. Listening to the crystal purity of the chant through her violent headache, she found herself meditating on the possibility of divine love in the midst of affliction.

"At a moment of intense physical pain," she wrote, "while I was making the effort to love, although believing I had no right to give any name to the love, I felt, while completely unprepared for it (I had never read the mystics), a presence more personal, more certain, and more real than that of a human being."

A moment later, she said, "Christ himself came down and took possession of me." Until then, she admitted, accounts of such experiences had put her off, but there was no denying what she was experiencing.

As an adolescent and a student, Weil had firmly dismissed the notion of God. The question of God was unanswerable, the problem insoluble. ("I decided that the only way of being sure not to reach a wrong solution, which seemed to me the greatest possible evil, was to leave it alone. So I left it alone.") So the reality of her adult experience caught her totally off guard: "In my arguments about the insolubility of the problem of God I had never foreseen the possibility of that, a real contact, person to person, here below, between a human being and God.... I had never read any mystical works because I had never felt any call to read them. God in his mercy had prevented me from reading the mystics, so that it should be evident to me that I had not invented this absolutely unexpected contact."

FOUND BY GOD

Even when she was younger, Simone Weil had been a great admirer of Blaise Pascal, although she'd always rejected his famous explanation of the human search for meaning—"You would not look for me if you had not already found me." Suddenly, however, the undeniable force of her own experience showed her that Pascal was right. We search only because of the insuppressible truth of God in us and around us and the unquenchable desire it creates. We find God only because we are found by God. St. Augustine had written centuries earlier, "I should not have sought you unless you had first found me."

Weil's story highlights another universal feature of the time for commitment—an unmistakable awareness that although we start out searching, we end up being discovered. We think we're looking for something, but we find that we're found by someone. The hound of heaven—to use the famous picture of Francis Thompson's poem—has tracked us down.

How can this be? How can we be fully ourselves in making the step of faith, while at the same time being decisively apprehended by God? Yet this is the almost universal experience in this fourth stage of the quest.

The same Masai warrior who saw faith as the lion's kill also knew the other side of the story. "You told us," he said to the European, "of the High God, how we must search for him, even leave our land and our people to find him. But we have not done this. We have not left our land. We have not searched for him. He has searched for us. He has searched us out and found us. All the time we think we are the lion. In the end, the lion is God."

THE REAL TERROR

When C. S. Lewis experienced the same thing, it terrified him. He knew his faith was "a perfectly free act." Yet he also felt his search getting out of hand. His neat philosophical distinction—between the idealist "Spirit" to which he was attracted and the "God of popular religion" he didn't want—was breaking down. People had spoken to him about faith as a comfort; he was discovering that "it does not begin in comfort; it begins in dismay."

For a start, Lewis wanted no interference in his life from anyone, and certainly not from God. "No word in my vocabulary expressed deeper hatred than the word *Interference*," he admits in *Surprised by Joy*. With his atheism so closely tied to his deep-seated mistrust of authority and his wish to be left alone, surrendering it would be costly. As he wrote in *The Problem of Pain*, "Rendering back one's will which we have so long claimed for our own, is, in itself, extraordinarily painful. To surrender a self-will inflamed and swollen with years of usurpation is a kind of death."

But what really arrested Lewis was the threat of life, not death. The theism he was coming to was not safely abstract and remote, an ideal he could admire yet control; it was suddenly alive and stirring. He'd developed the analogy that if ever Shakespeare and Hamlet were ever to meet, "it must be Shakespeare's doing. Hamlet could initiate nothing." But now the analogy closed on him like a mousetrap: "The real terror was that if you believed in even such a 'God' or 'Spirit' as I admitted, a wholly new situation developed. As the dry bones shook and came together in that dreadful valley of Ezekiel's, so now a philosophical theorem, cerebrally entertained, began to stir and heave and throw off its grave clothes, and stood upright and became a living presence. I was to be allowed to play at philosophy no longer. It might, as I say, still be true that my 'Spirit' was different in some way from 'the God of popular religion.' My Adversary waived the point. It sank into utter unimportance. He would not argue about it. He only said, 'I am the Lord'; 'I am that I am'; 'I am.'"

People who are naturally religious, Lewis went on, simply don't understand the horror of this situation. Nor do amiable agnostics who talk cheerfully about the search for God. "To me, as I then was, they might as well have talked about the mouse's search for the cat." But there was no turning back. The person he faced demanded total surrender.

"You must picture me alone," Lewis wrote, "in that room in Magdalen, night after night, feeling, whenever my mind lifted even for a second from my work, the steady, unrelenting approach of Him whom I so earnestly desired not to meet. That which I greatly feared had at last come upon me. In the Trinity Term of 1929 I gave in and admitted that God was God, and knelt and prayed: perhaps, that night, the most dejected and reluctant convert in all England."

DIFFERENT GOALS, DIFFERENT MEANS

This awareness of God's intervention is not only decisive for faith, it alters the entire perspective from which followers of Jesus Christ see the quest for meaning. Our previous look at our responsibility in faith was important—above all in underscoring beyond question that the search is more than a rational exercise; it's a personal journey. But recognizing God's part in our faith goes far beyond that. It casts the whole quest in a unique, new light that has no parallels in other faiths and philosophies.

The uniqueness of the biblical view of the quest lies in its estimate of the human ascent toward truth. In most faiths and philosophies, the quest is the "great ascent" of seekers toward their desired goals. For the Greeks and much of the ancient world, for example, *eros* was the way of love as desire, yearning, or appetite aroused by the attractive qualities of the object of its desire—whether honor, recognition, truth, justice, beauty, love, or God. To seek is therefore to long to love, and to direct one's desire and love to an object through which, in possessing it, one expects to become happy. Seeking is loving, which becomes desiring, which becomes possessing, which becomes happiness. For experience shows that in some way, "we all want to be happy," as Cicero said in *Hortensius*, and reasonable thought would indicate that the greatest happiness comes in possessing the greatest good.

Central to this view of the search—and also to its Hindu and Buddhist counterparts—is the conviction that the ascent is achievable. Given the required effort of mind or will, the seeker can make it to the good. The mountain is climbable. The summit is within human reach.

For the biblical faiths, by contrast, the insistence on God's part in faith is the decisive veto to such confidence. The way of *eros* only goes so far; to trust to human strength and desire alone is a formula for an inconclusive journey and an abortive quest. The only hope of success is the way of love as *agape* rather than *eros*. From this rival perspective, the secret of the search is not our "great ascent" but "the great descent"—of God toward us. Instead of the seeker finding love, love seeks out the seeker—not because the seeker is worthy of love but simply because love's nature is to love regardless of the worthiness or merit of the one loved.

The biblical view agrees with both the Greek and Eastern views that desire is at the very core of human existence. It goes on to side with the Greek view (over against the Eastern) in believing that desire itself is, or can be, good rather than evil; the legitimacy of the desire depends on the legitimacy of the object desired.

But the biblical way of *agape* breaks sharply with the way of *eros* at two points—the goals and the means of the search. First, the way of *agape* says, "By all means love, by all means desire, but consider carefully *what* you love and *what* you desire." The very fact that we desire is proof that we are creatures. We're incomplete in ourselves, so we desire whatever we think is beckoning to complete us.

We're therefore right to desire happiness but wrong to think that happiness may be found wherever our desires lead us. Only the true God can satisfy desire, for God alone needs nothing outside himself; he himself is the highest and the only lasting good. So all objects we desire, short of God, are either false (because they're unreal) or as finite and incomplete as we ourselves are—and therefore disappointing, if we make them the objects of ultimate desire.

True satisfaction and real rest can be found only in the highest and most lasting good, so all seeking short of the pursuit of God brings only restlessness. As St. Augustine confessed to him, "You have made us for yourself, and our hearts are restless until they find their rest in you."

The biblical way of *agape* also parts company with the way of *eros* over the means of the search. Considering the gulf between the creature and the Creator, no seeker—however dedicated, brilliant, virtuous, and tireless—can hope to bridge it. We cannot find God without God. We cannot reach God without God. We cannot satisfy God without God—which is another way of saying that all our seeking will always fall short unless God starts and finishes the search. The unaided search will always be forlorn.

In sum, the decisive part of our seeking is not our human ascent to God, but his descent to us. Without God's descent there is no human ascent. The secret of the quest lies not in our brilliance but in his grace. What puts us on the way is not the daring and ingenuity of our discovery of paths, but the disclosure of the one who has preceded us on all our paths.

BECAUSE HE WANTS YOU

At this stage of the journey we realize our need to do more than change a little or even a lot. We need the complete change that conversion brings. Like Plato's prisoners in the cave whose heads need to be turned if they are to escape from the shadows to the sun, or Saul on the road to Damascus, or Simone Weil in pursuit of truth, we all need the complete turnaround of conversion that leads us in the right direction.

And like the first disciples on the road with Jesus, or Dante on his journey through the circles of hell with Virgil, or Bunyan's Pilgrim on his progress toward the heavenly city, we all need a guide.

But both the reality of complete conversion and the provision of a sure guide are possible only because of the part God plays. "Continue seeking Him with seriousness," C. S. Lewis wrote in a letter. "Unless he wanted you, you would not be wanting him." As he had experienced in 1929, and as his wife, Joy Davidman, discovered later, the crucial event for the seeker is the decisive moment when "God came in."

———

Does your search still have the air of the remote and abstract? Or is there a stirring and a sense of something becoming real? Are you still in complete control of your search? Or are you finding yourself called into question by something or someone far bigger than yourself?

Let your heart and mind run deep. Engage with every fiber of your being on the long journey home.

TRUTH OR NOTHING

Henrik Ibsen's *Ghosts* is a play that shocked its original audience in Norway in 1881 and many others since then. But surely not many have fainted outright on seeing it as the eminent art historian Kenneth Clark did. And not just once but twice—first as a schoolboy at Winchester College, then many years later while viewing a production at London's National Theatre.

The play is the story of a young artist, Oswald Alving, who returns from Paris to spend the winter with his widowed mother. She's about to open an orphanage in memory of her husband, Oswald's father, who died ten years earlier. Slowly Oswald becomes aware that the father he has been brought up to revere had been a scoundrel and had lived a profligate life (their serving girl, Regina, was actually Captain Alving's illegitimate daughter). Oswald discovers also that he's beginning to go insane because of syphilis inherited from his father.

Mrs. Alving is forced to see her own part in this tragedy, but she is remorseless, having based all her actions on duty. The "ghosts" are the dead conventions and beliefs that led her to deny love and conceal the truth and that kept her from living "for the joy of life." "It is not only what we have inherited from our fathers and mothers that exists again in us," she says, "but all sorts of old ideas and all kinds of old dead beliefs.... And we are so miserably afraid of the light, all of us."

Oswald, the victim of his father's sins, is prepared for the onset of madness. But he urges his mother to give him a lethal dose of morphine because "I never asked you for life. And what kind of life was it that you gave me? I don't want it. You shall take it back!"

Recounting years later his fainting, Kenneth Clark could not remember at what point in the play he passed out the first time. But the second time it was the terrible ending that literally knocked him flat. Memories of his own childhood crashed in. Clark had grown up feeling both neglected and torn in two, pulled between his rich, dissolute, and irascible father and his dutiful but unemotional mother. Suddenly the weight of his inheritance felt unendurable, and he fainted with horror.

EGG-BOXING

The account of such incidents came as a surprise to many readers of Clark's biographies. They were such a contrast to the public image of Lord Clark, known for his encyclopedic wisdom, his urbane sophistication, his elegant manner. He was unrivaled in his day as an art historian and critic—London's answer to the artistic prominence of Paris. He was the youngest-ever director of the National Gallery and the man who saved his nation's art collections during the war. He was an influential author, his country's most brilliant lecturer, and a television performer acclaimed throughout the world for the BBC series *Civi-*

lization. He was one of the most admired, discussed, and envied men of his generation, as he pursued his mission to "bring art to the masses," or at least to bridge the gap between the refined taste of the few and the vast artistic ignorance of the many.

Kenneth Clark was all these things and more, a man of towering success. But few knew the other side of his personality and the immense cost to him of keeping hidden, even from himself, his strain of melancholy and his childhood sense of neglect. He was described as "six men in search of a character" by *New Statesman* magazine. "I don't really know K," Clark's friend, Graham Sutherland, remarked to another friend, who replied, "None of us do."

Sutherland, an eminent painter, tried later to capture Clark in a portrait. K, as Kenneth Clark was known to his friends, considered this an honor and enjoyed the sittings. But Sutherland was never satisfied and finally gave up, just as other artists did who tried to paint him. Clark was too mercurial to be pinned down. His expressions flickered constantly, and the painter never knew which inner person the sitter wanted to convey.

Seen from this fuller perspective, Kenneth Clark's urbanity was a mask and a protective device, as was the ironic detachment and self-deprecation that became his signature style. For writing his autobiography, he spoke of having "discovered a tone of voice, detached and slightly ironical, that I could use throughout the whole book." Others, however, had detected this tone much earlier. A contemporary at Winchester called it his "Curzonian superiority"; another at Oxford said that Clark's precocious learning and sophistication made him seem more like a don of forty than an undergraduate.

Clark of course saw himself differently in those school years: "I cannot belong to a group. Although I have been elected to nine clubs and have paid the entrance fees, I have resigned from all but one simply because I have been too embarrassed to speak to any of the members." A close friend noted that although Clark at this time was often "writing himself off," he would react angrily and defensively if anyone else did.

Some reviewers of *The Other Half,* the second volume of Clark's autobiography, saw demons below the surface of his urbanity. Christopher Booker wrote, "As the picture of a man who has never to the end dared to face up to 'the other half' of himself, this is a spine-chilling book." But Clark's friends were kinder and more understanding, recognizing that he had evolved protective devices to insulate himself. One of them was his way of compartmentalizing various aspects of his life. This "egg-boxing," as one friend called it, allowed him to keep safely separate such things as his darker childhood memories and his involvement with several mistresses.

THE AWKWARD PROBLEM

Perhaps this device helps explain Clark's well-known response to religion. To be sure, there had been no religious example or instruction in his early life. His mother—who was sexually inhibited, never laughed, and was unable to express her feelings—feared going to church because it might touch her emotions. The impetus toward faith in Clark's life came from elsewhere, especially from three things that mattered most to him—his deep love of nature (this gave him his first religious experience as a child), his passion for art, and his eventual conviction that the nobility of civilization could not survive without spiritual roots.

Clark went through recurring religious experiences and did not doubt that they were genuine. One came while working on a book in a hotel room in Aldeburgh, Suffolk, near his childhood home. Just as he finished writing a passage on Rubens, he realized he was shaking vehemently from his touch with the power of creativity, so much so that he had to go out and walk along the sea front to calm himself. Clearly, artistic inspiration and spiritual illumination were only a hairsbreadth apart. "I make no claim to be an inspired writer," he noted later, "but I know what inspiration feels like, which makes it easier for me, as a critic, to recognize it in others."

Shortly afterward, working on the same book, he was staying as the guest of Bernard Berenson at the Villa i Tatti in Florence (where Bertrand Russell had written his essay on "A Free Man's Worship"). "I lived in solitude," Clark recalled later, "surrounded by books on the history of religion, which have always been my favourite reading." This, he thought, might help explain "a curious episode" that he recounted:

"I had a religious experience. It took place in the Church of San Lorenzo, but did not seem to be connected with the harmonious beauty of the architecture. I can only say that for a few minutes my whole being was irradiated by a kind of heavenly joy, far more intense than anything I had known before. This state of mind lasted for several months, and, wonderful though it was, it posed an awkward problem in terms of action. My life was far from blameless: I would have to reform. My family would think I was going mad, and perhaps after all, it *was* a delusion, for I was in every way unworthy of receiving such a flood of grace. Gradually the effect wore off, and I made no effort to retain it. I think I was right; I was too deeply embedded in the world to change course. But that I had 'felt the finger of God' I am quite sure, and, although the memory of this experience has faded, it still helps me to understand the joys of the saints."

From these words, two conclusions are undeniable—that Clark was quite sure he "had felt the finger of God," and that he had equally and decisively declined to respond to it, so that the memory of the experience finally paled.

Later, after many conversations with a deeply intellectual Christian friend who never tried to convert him, Clark simply remarked: "He only went as far as to say that he knew I was looking for something. So I was, and still am."

As with so many of his secrets, the conclusion to Kenneth Clark's journey would come out only after his death in May 1985. His memorial service at St. James' Piccadilly was a grand affair, with many of the world's intellectual and cultural elite present. They were stunned by an address from an Irish priest, who recounted that Clark had made his confession and been received into the church a week before he died. "This great man then said to me, 'Thank you, Father! You have done for me what I have long been wanting.'"

The stir among Clark's friends was considerable. Deathbed conversions can be troubling because of the potential for manipulation and fabrication. But Lady Clark said the report was accurate; her husband's commitment of faith had been secret but longstanding. At the close of his life, he had grasped the hand of God that he earlier brushed aside.

YOUR KNEES OR YOUR HEELS?

Kenneth Clark's story highlights another critical component in the fourth phase of the quest: The truth may be pressing, conclusions may be compelling, but there's no inevitability of faith and commitment even at this point. We are free people, and there are always two options before us—to fall on our knees or to turn on our heels.

Such a moment tests and exposes the honesty of our search as seekers. Either we may seek to conform our desires to the truth, which leads to conviction, or we may seek to conform the truth to our desires, which leads to evasions.

Nietzsche used the term "danger point" for the moment when people fully recognize the desperate conclusion of nihilism—that there's no meaning in life; he then noted how many fail to face the conclusion squarely and instead twist and turn. A more precise danger point is the moment when searchers finally see the truth of faith, and yet many still try to evade its logic and sidestep its force. Like a yachtsman changing tack or a cornered boxer bouncing off the ropes, they duck the issue, perhaps putting out a smoke screen of excuses and evasions—often highly contradictory.

Such contradiction, so common, is something G. K. Chesterton observed: "One rationalist had hardly done calling Christianity a nightmare before another began to call it a fool's paradise. This puzzled me; the charges seemed inconsistent. Christianity could not at once be the black mask on a white world or a white mask on a black world. The state of the Christian could not be at once so comfortable that he was a coward to cling to it, and so uncomfortable that he was a fool to stand it."

C. S. Lewis saw the same smoke screens in skeptics: "Such people put up a version of Christianity suitable for a child of six and make that the object of their attack. When you try and explain the Christian doctrine as it is really held by an instructed adult, they then complain that you are making their heads turn around and that it is all too complicated and that if there really was a God they are sure He would have made 'religion' simple."

Lewis observed inconsistencies in his own quest as well, and they were much more personal and emotional. He confessed in *Surprised by Joy*: "I was at this time living, like so many atheists or anti-theists, in a whirl of contradictions. I maintained that God did *not* exist. I was also very angry with God for not existing. I was equally angry with him for creating a world."

Such a welter of conflicting thoughts and emotions is common at this moment of truth, but it doesn't last. A spinning coin cannot spin forever. Nor can our minds remain undecided forever, since not to decide is itself a decision. And as the coin will come down only heads or tails, so we also have only two options, not three or more. Either we conform our desires to the truth or we conform the truth to our desires.

The blunt challenge of this choice flies in the face of the modern myth that human beings are by nature truth seekers whose sole motto, in Max Weber's words, is "truth or nothing." Instead, our honestly assessed experience underscores what the biblical faiths have taught all along: As human beings we're by nature truth seekers; as fallen human beings we're also by nature truth twisters. For each person who genuinely cries, "Truth or nothing," a thousand others in the crunch will say, "Anything but truth!" As the French filmmaker François Truffaut admitted, "There is in me a refusal to learn that is as powerful as my desire to know."

In his book *People of the Lie*, Scott Peck tells of counseling sessions with a woman named Charlene. "Everything seems meaningless," she complained repeatedly. His deeper probing revealed that she was a religious person with a well-developed religious world-view, who had actually taught her religious beliefs professionally for two years. Why then, Peck asked, did those beliefs not make a difference to her sense of meaninglessness?

There was a short silence. Then she exploded: "I cannot do it. There's not room for *me* in that. That would be my death. I don't want to live for God. I will not. I want to live for me. My own sake!"

TRUTH TWISTING

Once again we face what we saw in earlier chapters but now in a different guise. Biography can overwhelm philosophy in the best of us. None of us has a steel-trap mind so dispassionate that we're pure truth seekers; all of us are truth twisters too. And the uncomfortable fact is that our mind is as much to blame for this as our emotions and our will. In fact, the cleverer the mind, the more slippery the heart. The more sophisticated the education, the subtler the rationalization. Sometimes erudition only lends conviction to self-deception, for no one is easier to deceive than ourselves.

Sometimes the rationalization is brazen. In his bizarre public confessional, *Ends and Means,* Aldous Huxley admitted that he "took it for granted" that the world had no meaning. "I had motives," he wrote, "for not wanting the world to have meaning. Consequently I assumed that it had none, and was able without any difficulty to find satisfying reason for this assumption." Huxley reached this view for what he acknowledged were "non-intellectual reasons" (what Pascal called "passions"). He then rationalized, providing reasons other than the real reasons. It was a classic case of what the French call "bad faith."

Huxley then dug his hole deeper: "It is our will that then decides how and upon what subject we shall use our intelligence." After all, he continued, "the philosopher who finds no meaning in the world is not concerned exclusively with a problem in metaphysics. He is also concerned to prove that there is no valid reason why he personally should not do as he wants, or why his friends should not seize political power and govern in the way they find most advantageous to themselves."

Huxley's irrationality is blatant. Bad faith, a self-serving projection, a life lie for him and his elite friends, an ideology (in his full-blown definition for that word: a set of ideas serving as a social weapon for his self-interests)—Huxley pleaded guilty on every count, then hammered his point home with a grand conclusion: "For myself, no doubt, as for most of my contemporaries, the philosophy of meaninglessness was essentially liberation from a certain political and economic system and liberation from a certain system of morality. We objected to the morality because it interfered with our sexual freedom."

Few people are as candid as Aldous Huxley, but he isn't alone. The great economist John Maynard Keynes described the position of his Bloomsbury Group as "immoralism"—"We repudiated entirely customary morals, conventions, and traditional wisdom"—and he claimed that their philosophy "was a very good one to grow up under." Beatrice Webb, the grande dame of Fabian socialism, deplored such a philosophy and its transparent motives: "I never see anything in it, except a metaphysical justification for doing what you like and what other people disapprove of."

SHORT TERM VERSUS LONG

The strategy of conforming the truth to our desires, although easier and more attractive in the short term, is harder in the long. Although it allows us to remain in control, the snag is that in leading us away from truth, it leads us away from reality and therefore requires endless evasions. Worse, because it takes us away from what is real and true, it inevitably ends in disappointment and lostness.

Conversely, the decision to conform our desires to the truth is harder in the short term but easier in the long. We give up our need for control and submit to truth outside us, a submission that requires repentance (if we were wrong about the truth before). We have to face up to reality rather than trying to fit reality into our schemes. But the long-term outcome is freedom, because truth *is* freedom as we engage with reality as it truly is.

In sum, this stage of the search reminds us again that there's a moral dimension to knowing. As we saw at the beginning, the seeker's quest for meaning is different from a miner's search for gold or a surveyor's exploration for oil. All are searching for a goal, but for the seeker, the openness to grow and change is a precondition for the successful discovery.

TRUTH'S CAPTIVE

Sigmund Freud once said he saw himself as essentially a conqueror: "I am actually not at all a man of science, not an observer, not an experimenter.... I am by temperament nothing but a *conquistador,* an adventurer." The seeker after truth, however, is not a conqueror but a supplicant. Because there's no one easier to deceive than ourselves, and no bigger credibility gap than that between our truth seeking and our truth twisting, our only path to truth (and its resultant freedom) is to be transformed by it rather than trying to conquer it.

We must conform to truth—or, more accurately, become captive to it. Ultimately the question for each of us is not how thoroughly we've searched for the truth but how searchingly the truth has examined us.

We started this book by seeing that the unexamined life is not worth living; we end by realizing that the untransformed life is not worthy of finding. As Kierkegaard wrote in *The Last Years*: "The truth is a snare; you cannot have it without being caught. You cannot have the truth in such a way that you catch it, but only in such a way that it catches you."

———

Is it "truth or nothing" for you in your search? Or is it "anything but truth"? Are you trying to conform the truth as you have found it to your desires as you know them? Or are you willing to conform your desires as you know them to the truth as you've found it?

Let your heart and mind run deep. Engage with every fiber of your being on the long journey home.

CHAPTER EIGHTEEN

ENTREPRENEURS OF LIFE

"As you know, I have been very fortunate in my career and I've made a lot of money—far more than I ever dreamed of, far more than I could ever spend, far more than my family needs." The speaker was a prominent businessman at a conference near Oxford University. The strength of his determination and character showed in his face, but a moment's hesitation betrayed deeper emotions hidden behind the outward intensity. A single tear rolled slowly down his well-tanned cheek.

"To be honest, one of my motives for making so much money was simple—to have the money to hire people to do what I don't like doing. But there's one thing I've never been able to hire anyone to do for me: find my own sense of purpose and fulfillment. I'd give anything to discover that."

A sense of purpose and fulfillment is the single strongest issue flowing out of the quest for meaning. Which leads us to the final

---

By design, and with the publisher's permission, this last chapter overlaps with the first chapter of *The Call*, so that *Long Journey Home* is the prelude to *The Call*.

point about this road map to the seeker's quest for meaning: The end of the quest for meaning is the beginning of the journey of faith. Indeed, nothing better illuminates the entire journey of life and faith, and in particular the special challenge of finishing well, than the issue of purpose.

SOMETHING DEFINITE

Our passion is to know we're fulfilling the purpose for which we're here on earth. We all desire to make a difference. We long to leave a legacy. We yearn, as Ralph Waldo Emerson put it, "to leave the world a bit better."

Our notions of how to do this differ enormously. Artists, scientists, and builders often labor to create a unique work that can live forever in their name. Politicians, businesspeople, and administrators usually think more in terms of institutions they've created and sustained. Parents, teachers, and counselors view their contribution in terms of lives shaped and matured. But for all the variety, the need for purpose is the same. As Thomas Carlyle wrote, "The man without a purpose is like a ship without a rudder—a waif, a nothing, a no-man."

All other standards of success—wealth, power, position, knowledge, friendships—grow tinny and hollow if we don't satisfy this deeper longing. For some people the hollowness leads to what Henry David Thoreau described as "lives of quiet desperation"; for others the emptiness and aimlessness deepen into a stronger despair.

In an early draft of Dostoevsky's *The Brothers Karamazov*, the Inquisitor gives a terrifying account of what happens to the human soul when it doubts its purpose: "For the secret of man's being is not only to live...but to live for something definite. Without a firm notion of what he is living for, man will not accept life and will rather destroy himself than remain on earth."

Call it the greatest good *(summum bonum)*, the ultimate end, or whatever you choose. But finding and fulfilling the purpose of our lives comes up in myriad ways and in all the seasons of our lives:

Teenagers feel it as the world of freedom beyond home and secondary school beckons with a dizzying range of choices.

Graduate students confront it when the excitement of "the world is my oyster" is chilled by the thought that opening up one choice means closing down others.

Those in their early thirties know it when their daily work assumes its own brute reality beyond their earlier considerations of the wishes of their parents, the fashions of their peers, and the allure of salary and career prospects.

People in midlife face it when a mismatch between their gifts and their work reminds them daily that they are square pegs in round holes. Can they see themselves "doing that for the rest of their lives"?

Mothers feel it when their children grow up, and they wonder which high purpose will fill the void in the next stage of their lives.

Successful people in their forties and fifties come up against it suddenly when their accomplishments raise questions concerning the social responsibility of their success and, deeper still, the purpose of their lives.

People confront it in all the varying transitions of the journey of life—from moving homes to switching jobs to breakdowns in marriage to crises of health. Negotiating these changes feels longer and worse than the changes themselves because transition challenges our sense of personal meaning.

Those in their later years often face it again. What does life add up to? Were the successes real? Were they worth the trade-offs? Having gained a whole world, however huge or tiny, have we sold our souls cheaply and missed the point of it all? As Walker Percy wrote, "You can get all A's and still flunk life."

Søren Kierkegaard was driven by the question of his life purpose. He realized that personal purpose isn't a matter of philosophy or theory. It isn't purely objective, and it isn't inherited like a legacy. Many a scientist has an encyclopedic knowledge of the world, many a philosopher can survey vast systems of thought, many a theologian can unpack the profundities of religion, and many a journalist can seemingly speak on any topic raised. But all that is theory and, without a sense of personal purpose, vanity.

Only a larger purpose—one that is for each of us personal and passionate—can inspire us to heights we know we could never reach on our own. Kierkegaard wrote in his *Journal*, "The thing is to understand myself, to see what God really wants *me* to do; the thing is to find a truth which is true *for me*, to find the *idea for which I can live and die*."

TOO MUCH TO LIVE WITH, TOO LITTLE TO LIVE FOR

In our own day this question of life purpose is more urgent than ever. Three factors have converged to fuel a search for significance without precedent in human history.

First, the search for the purpose of life is one of the deepest issues of our experiences as human beings. Second, the expectation that we can all live purposeful lives has been given a gigantic boost by modern society's offer of the maximum opportunity for choice and change in all we do. Third, our fulfillment is thwarted by this stunning fact: Out of more than a score of great civilizations in human history, modern Western civilization is the very first to have no agreed-on answer to the question of the purpose of life.

More ignorance, confusion, and longing surround this topic now than at almost any time in history. The trouble is that, as modern people, we have too much to live with and too little to live for. Some feel they have time but not enough money; others feel they have money but not enough time. Most of us, in the midst of material plenty, have spiritual poverty.

The ironies don't stop there. Consider the fact that modern science brings us closer and closer to the extraordinary design in the universe, yet modern people shy away from discovering purpose in individual lives. Or the fact that a consensus is emerging on the human "life course," but there's no corresponding agreement on the purpose of lives that follow this course.

Part of the confusion stems from the conflicting views of purpose on offer today. In essence the Eastern faiths say, "Forget it"—the very desire for purpose is a craving that traps us in the world of illusion. The Western secularist faiths say, "Do it your own way"—purpose must be created rather than discovered, because there's no design for our individual lives any more than the universe has any special design for humanity. And the biblical faiths say, "Follow the call of your Creator"—there's no greater purpose and fulfillment for anyone than in discovering and living out the design for which God created us and sent us into the world.

In the absence of consensus, many people simply make do by muddling along as best they can.

A KNOWN DESTINATION

The confusion is compounded by conflicting views of life as a journey. At one extreme are those who shun that picture and speak as if they've arrived. They properly emphasize the certainties and triumphs of faith, but they minimize the uncertainties and tragedies. All truths are clear-cut, all hopes materialized, all conclusions foregone—and all sense of journeying is reduced to the vanishing point. There are seemingly no risks, trials, dangers, setbacks, or disasters on their horizon.

Sadly, they forget that life is a pilgrim's progress. As the celebrated Rabbi Kotzker said, "He who thinks he is finished *is* finished."

At the other extreme are those for whom journeying without end becomes a passion and a way of life. To them it's unthinkable ever to arrive, and the ultimate gaucherie is to claim to have found a way or reached a conclusion. The journey itself is all. Questions, inquiry, searching, and conquering become ends in themselves. Ambiguity is everything.

Sadly for them, they refuse to find what they're looking for. As Daniel Boorstin, the librarian of Congress, remarked, "We have come from seeking meaning to finding meaning in the seeking."

Thoughtful people in the modern world are more prone to this second problem. There have always been insatiable searchers, such as Dr. Faust, but never has eternal restlessness been as common as it is today, especially as it is stoked by consumerism. When we're moving, we dream of rest; when we rest, we dream of moving again. When we have little, we dream of more; when we have much, we dream of even more. The grammar of our forward-thrusting desires has no periods or paragraph endings—only commas and an endless series of "howevers" and "on the other hands."

For thinkers in the modern consumer world, no less than for modern shoppers, desire is allowed to desire only desire. To keep the system going, desire is stimulated to desire anything and everything except satisfaction. After all, compared with the cornucopia of choices coming, you haven't seen anything yet, so it would be foolish to make a choice now. Life in this view is never a crossroads but a cafeteria of endless choices.

Traditional societies were often trapped by their past into succumbing to stagnation. We modern people are lured by the future into yielding to the restlessness of perpetual craving. Like the story of the Flying Dutchman, we're compelled to roam the seas under a perpetual, self-inflicted damnation. We rightly celebrate free inquiry and open-ended thinking while we drown out the problems of our loss of direction, our loss of a rudder, our loss of a map, and most important, our loss of home.

Again the Christian faith maintains an extraordinary balance between the siren pull of these extremes. We're on a journey, so we're truly travelers, with all the attendant costs, risks, and dangers of traveling. Never in this life can we say we've arrived. But we know why we've lost our original home and, more important, we know the home to which we're going, the one who awaits us there, and the one who goes with us on the journey.

To those who say, "The search is its own reward" or "Better to travel hopefully than arrive," followers of Jesus respond that a journey is meaningful only if it has a destination; traveling hopefully is possible only if we're traveling homeward. So all who follow Jesus are wayfarers but not wanderers. They haven't arrived, but they have found the way. In knowing the one who first navigated the journey, they've found the one who *is* the way, the truth, and the life. Down the centuries and across all continents, they are, in the words of St. Augustine, "a society of pilgrims of all languages."

VISIONARIES WHO ADD VALUE

How then do we travel the journey purposefully and finish well? The way to make the most of the journey of life and faith is to answer the call of our Creator, and in so doing discover the purpose for which we were created and to which we're called. The great Creator alone creates completely out of nothing—fruitfully and prolifically. He alone knows our reason for being, by which he calls us into a life of purpose. As we rise to our Creator's call, we become subcreators made in his image, and we enter into our own creativity, artistry, and entrepreneurship, thus adding to the rich fruitfulness of the universe in the course of our lives on earth. Answering the call of our Creator is therefore the highest source of purpose on the journey. It transforms us into "entrepreneurs of life" on the long journey home.

Today the term "creator" is often restricted to artists and the term "entrepreneur" to businesspeople, but as we live life by faith, we're all creators, we're all artists, we're all entrepreneurs. This is at the very heart of our calling as human beings.

At least it's becoming clearer in our age that human purpose cannot be found in means, but only in ends. Capitalism, for all its creativity and fruitfulness, falls short when challenged to answer the question "Why?" By itself it's literally meaningless in that it's only a mechanism, not a source of meaning. So too are politics, science, psychology, management, self-help techniques, and a host of other modern theories. What Tolstoy wrote of science applies to all of them:

"Science is meaningless because it gives no answer to our question, the only question important to us, 'what shall we do and how shall we live?'" There is no answer outside the deeper quest for faith, and no implication of faith is deeper and more satisfying than answering the call.

What is meant by "calling"? Simply that God calls us to himself so decisively that everything we are, everything we do, and everything we have is invested with a special devotion and dynamism lived out as a response to his summons and service.

And what is meant by "entrepreneurs of life"? They are those who assume responsibility for a creative task, not as an assigned role, a routine function, or an inherited duty, but as a venture of faith, including risk and danger, in order to bring into the world something new and profitable to humankind. This is their calling. And by answering such a call, by rising to it in faith, entrepreneurs of life use their talents and resources to be fruitful and to bring added value into the world as they journey. They quite literally make the invisible visible, the future present, the ideal real, the impossible an achievement, the desired an experience, the status quo dynamic, and the dream a fulfillment.

To be sure, there's much in life we did not choose and cannot change. At the beginning of life none of us decided the date of our birth, the color of our eyes, or the pedigree of our ancestry. At the end of life we will not decide the day of our death or the interpretation of our legacy. And in between there are a million and one circumstances over which we have no control. But we're still, always, essentially people of significance—men and women whose entrepreneurial capacity to exercise dominion, assert influence, and multiply fruitfulness is at the heart of our humanness and the secret to making the most of our journey of life.

This stress on the entrepreneurial must not be confused with the heartless attitude that values people only when they are productive. But it's a reminder, as Dallas Willard writes, that all of us have "a unique eternal calling to count for good in God's great universe."

This truth—the call to be followers of the way, with the entrepreneurial vision and energy it provides—has been a driving force in many of the greatest "leaps forward" in history: the constitution of the Jewish nation at Mount Sinai, the birth of the Christian movement in Galilee, the sixteenth-century Reformation and its incalculable impetus to the rise of the modern world, and the abolition of slavery and the slave trade in the West, to name a few. Little wonder that the rediscovery of calling should be critical today in satisfying the passion for purpose within millions of questing modern people.

A MOTIVE FOR A LIFETIME

Do you long to build on the commitment faith, to discover your sense of purpose, to engage life on the journey as an entrepreneurial life task? A sense of calling can be your central motive in this mission. T. S. Eliot asked, "Can a lifetime represent a single motive?" If the single motive is simply our own, the answer must be no. We aren't wise enough, pure enough, or strong enough to aim and sustain such a single motive over the journey of a lifetime. That way lies fanaticism or failure.

But if the single motive is the master motive of God's calling, the answer is yes. In any and all situations on the road, both today and tomorrow, God's call is our unchanging and ultimate what, why, and whither.

In times of faith, Alexis de Tocqueville observed, "the final aim of life is placed beyond life." That's what calling does to the journey. "Follow me," Jesus said two thousand years ago and changed the course of history. That's why calling provides the Archimedean point by which faith moves the world. That's why calling is the most comprehensive reorientation and the most profound motivation on the human journey. Answering the call is the way to find and fulfill the central, entrepreneurial purpose of your life as you journey home.

In one of his letters Vincent van Gogh described a painting he'd seen depicting John Bunyan's *Pilgrim's Progress*. A sandy path leads over the hills to a mountain, on top of which is the Heavenly City. On the road is a pilgrim who wants to go to the city. But he's tired and turns to a woman standing beside the road and asks:

"Does the road go uphill all the way?"

"Yes, to the very end."

"And will the journey take all day long?"

"Yes, from morn till night, my friend."

"Truly," van Gogh concluded, "it is not a picture, but an inspiration." For uphill though the way may often wind, and hard though the road may sometimes be, what lies ahead at the journey's end is home. This is the homecoming to which all restless hearts are invited. "There shall we rest and see, see and love, love and praise," Augustine wrote in *The City of God*. "This is what we shall be in the end without end. For what other end do we propose to ourselves than to attain to the kingdom of which there is no end?"

No less than that is the goal and the reward of the search. Is it not time to find and follow the way and, one day, to finish well on the long journey home?

GRATEFUL
ACKNOWLEDGMENTS

One of the benefits of being an occasional writer is a vivid awareness of the debts of gratitude to those without whom there would be no writing at all. This book owes a deep debt to the following:

To St. Augustine, Blaise Pascal, Fyodor Dostoevsky, G. K. Chesterton, C. S. Lewis, Francis Schaeffer, and Peter L. Berger, whose thoughts and writings are major signposts on my own journey home.

To Professor Peter Feaver of Duke University and Kelly Monroe and the Veritas Forum committees of the Universities of Michigan, Berkeley, Stanford, Florida, Penn State, UCLA, and Santa Barbara, whose kind invitations gave me the occasion to develop these ideas.

To Paul Klaassen and the trustees of the Trinity Forum, and to my wonderful colleagues Steve Haas, Jonathan Butcher, Amos Good, Ginger Koloszyc, Greta Liesenfelt, Mike Metzger, Boyd Moore, John and Carol Nothwang, Carrie Smith, and Jeff Wright, who give me the time and space to write in the midst of our hectic schedules.

To Debi Siler, whose genius at deciphering my indecipherable handwriting is legendary and whose enthusiasm and cheerfulness is infectious.

To Ralph Crosby and Bill Edgar, whose tough but friendly reviews of the first draft saved me from numerous blunders and set me on my way to the present manuscript.

To Dan Rich and Thomas Womack of WaterBrook and Eric Major of Doubleday, and their colleagues in both houses, whose experience and skills made the process of publishing a genuine marvel and pleasure.

We want to hear from you. Please send your comments about this
book to us in care of the address below. Thank you.

ZONDERVAN™

GRAND RAPIDS, MICHIGAN 49530 USA

WWW.ZONDERVAN.COM